Wise Men Talking Series

HAN FEI ZI
韩非子说 Says

蔡希勤 编注

□ 责任编辑 韩颖
□ 翻译 韩芙芸
□ 绘图 李士伋

老人家说系列丛书

华语教学出版社
SINOLINGUA

First Edition 2012

ISBN 978-7-5138-0143-0
Copyright 2012 by Sinolingua
Published by Sinolingua
24 Baiwanzhuang Road, Beijing 100037, China
Tel: (86)10- 68320585   68997826
Fax: (86)10- 68997826   68326333
http://www.sinolingua.com.cn
E-mail: hyjx@sinolingua.com.cn
Printed by Beijing Songyuan Printing Co., Ltd.

Printed in the People's Republic of China

老人家说

俗曰:"不听老人言,吃亏在眼前。"

老人家走的路多,吃的饭多,看的书多,经的事多,享的福多,受的罪多,可谓见多识广,有丰富的生活经验,老人家说的话多是经验之谈,后生小子不可不听也。

在中国历史上,春秋战国时期是中国古代思想高度发展的时期,那个时候诸子并起,百家争鸣,出现了很多"子"字辈的老人家,他们有道家、儒家、墨家、名家、法家、兵家、阴阳家,多不胜数,车载斗量,一时星河灿烂。

后来各家各派的代表曾先后聚集于齐国稷下学宫。齐宣王是个开明的诸侯王,因纳无盐丑女钟离春为后而名声大噪。他对各国来讲学的专家学者不问来路一律管吃管住,给予政府津贴。对愿留下来做官的,授之以客卿,造巨室,付万钟;对不愿做官的,也给予"不治事而议论"之特殊待遇。果然这些人各为其主,各为其派,百家争鸣,百花齐放,设坛辩论,著书立说:有的说仁,有的说义,有的说无为,有的说逍遥,有的说非攻,有的说谋攻,有的说性善,有的说性恶,有的说亲非亲,有的说马非马,知彼知己,仁者无敌……留下了很多光辉灿烂的学术经典。

可惜好景不长,秦始皇时丞相李斯递话说"焚书坑儒",结果除秦记、医药、卜筮、种树书外,民间所藏诗、书及百家典籍均被一把火烧个精光。到西汉武帝时,董仲舒又上书提出"罢黜百家,独尊儒术",从此,儒学成了正统,"黄老、刑名百家之言"成为邪说。

"有德者必有言",儒学以外的各家各派虽屡被扫荡,却不断变换着生存方式以求不灭,并为我们保存下了十分丰富的经典著作。在这些经典里,先哲们留下了很多充满智慧和哲理的、至今仍然熠熠发光的至理名言,我们将这些各家各派的老人家的"金玉良言"编辑成这套《老人家说》丛书,加以注释并译成英文,采取汉英对照方式出版,以飨海内外有心有意于中国传统文化的广大读者。

As the saying goes, "If an old dog barks, he gives counsel."

Old men, who walk more roads, eat more rice, read more books, have more experiences, enjoy more happiness, and endure more sufferings, are experienced and knowledgeable, with rich life experience. Thus, what they say is mostly wise counsel, and young people should listen to them.

The Spring and Autumn (770-476 BC) and Warring States (475-221 BC) periods of Chinese history were a golden age for ancient Chinese thought. In those periods, various schools of thought, together with many sages whose names bore the honorific suffix " Zi, " emerged and contended, including the Taoist school, Confucian school, Mohist school, school of Logicians, Legalist school, Military school and Yin-Yang school. Numerous and well known, these schools of thought were as brilliant as the Milky Way.

Later representatives of these schools of thought flocked to the Jixia Academy of the State of Qi. Duke Xuan of Qi was an enlightened ruler, famous for making an ugly but brilliant woman his wife. The duke provided board and lodging, as well as government subsidies for experts and scholars coming to give lectures, and never inquired about their backgrounds. For those willing to hold official positions, the duke appointed them guest officials, built mansions for them and paid them high salaries. Those unwilling to take up official posts were kept on as advisors. This was an era when " one hundred schools of thought contended and a hundred flowers blossomed. " The scholars debated in forums, and wrote books to expound their doctrines: Some preached benevolence; some, righteousness; some, inaction; some, absolute freedom; some, aversion to offensive war; some, attack by stratagem; some, the goodness of man's nature; some, the evil nature of man. Some said that relatives were not relatives; some said that horses were not horses; some urged the importance of knowing oneself and one's enemy; some said that benevolence knew no enemy .... And they left behind many splendid classic works of scholarship.

Unfortunately, this situation did not last long. When Qin Shihuang (reigned 221-210 BC) united all the states of China, and ruled as the First Emperor, his prime minister, Li Si, ordered that all books except those on medicine, fortune telling and tree planting be burned. So, all poetry collections and the classics of the various schools of thought were destroyed. Emperor Wu (reigned 140-88BC) of the Western Han Dynasty made Confucianism the orthodox doctrine of the state, while other schools of thought, including the Taoist and Legalist schools, were deemed heretical.

These other schools, however, managed to survive, and an abundance of their classical works have been handed down to us. These classical works contain many wise sayings and profound insights into philosophical theory which are still worthy of study today. We have compiled these nuggets of wisdom uttered by old men of the various ancient schools of thought into this series Wise Men Talking, and added explanatory notes and English translation for the benefit of both Chinese and overseas readers fond of traditional Chinese culture.

目录
CONTENTS

1

are distant and humble.

聪明睿智，天也〔10〕

The hearing, sight and intelligence of man are endowed by nature.

D

大不可量，深不可测〔12〕

The emperor's governing skill is too great to be measured and too profound to be surveyed.

大费无罪而少得为功〔14〕

If those who waste large sums of money receive no punishment and those who make small achievements are rewarded ...

耽于女乐，不顾国政〔16〕

A country's downfall begins if the emperor indulges in carnal pleasures and neglects state affairs.

道譬诸若水，溺者多饮之即死〔18〕

Tao can be compared to water. The drowned die from drinking too much ...

道在不可见，用在不可知〔20〕

Tao is invisible, thus no one knows when the emperor employs it.

道者，万物之始，是非之纪也〔22〕

Tao is the beginning point of all lives and the source of right and wrong.

得天时，则不务而自生〔24〕

At the right time, the crops will flourish without great effort.

德也者，人之所以建生也〔26〕

Morality is the root of existence.

F

罚薄不为慈，诛严不为戾〔28〕

It is not an act of charity to administer light penalties, nor is it an act of cruelty to enforce strict ones.

法败则国乱，民怨则国危〔30〕

If laws are not obeyed, the country will be in chaos. If the people exist in hatred, the country will be in danger.

法不阿贵，绳不挠曲〔32〕

Laws do not favor the ministers in power, just as an ink marker does not make a curved line on its own.

法莫如显，而术不欲见〔34〕

Laws should be made clear and public, while the methods of ruling the subordinates should be kept hidden.

夫虎之所以能服狗者，爪牙也〔36〕

A tiger can overcome a dog by virtue of its claws and teeth.

夫使民有功与无功俱赏者〔38〕

If both people of merit and demerit are equally rewarded ...

夫物者有所宜，材者有所施〔40〕

Just as all things have different functions, all people are endowed

with special talents.

凡治天下，必因人情〔42〕

When governing a country, the ruler should take worldly wisdom

into consideration.

G

功当其事，事当其言，则赏〔44〕

Ministers whose accomplishments equal their words should be

rewarded.

工匠不得施其技巧，故屋坏弓折〔46〕

If artisans are not able to utilize their skills, houses will fall and

bows will break.

H

火形严，故人鲜灼〔48〕

As fire seems frightening, people escape from it and seldom are

burned.

祸难生于邪心，邪心诱于可欲〔50〕

Disasters grow out of evil thoughts. Evil thoughts are induced by greed.

今欲以先王之政，治当世之民〔52〕

If we adhere to the ruling system of previous kings to govern the current people . . .

禁奸之法，太上禁其心〔54〕

Among the methods of suppressing evil deeds, the best is to curb the wicked mind.

镜无见疵之罪，道无明过之怨〔56〕

As mirror should not be punished due to its reflection of flaws, Tao should not be hated because of its exposure of wrong doings.

君无见其所欲〔58〕

The sovereign should not expose his preferences.

君有道，则臣尽力而奸不生〔60〕

If the sovereign adopts the right ruling system, his ministers will exert themselves to their utmost, and evil will not arise.

离朱易百步而难眉睫〔62〕

Li Zhu could see a hair from a distance as far away as a hundred steps, yet not see his own eyebrows and lashes.

吏者，民之本，纲者也〔64〕

The officials are the roots of the people.

盲则不能避昼日之险〔66〕

As a blind man cannot avoid danger in daylight ...

名实相持而成，形影相应而立〔68〕

Names and reality depend upon each other; form and shadow are opposites.

明夫恃人不如自恃也〔70〕

Everyone should understand that relying on oneself is better than relying upon others.

明君无偷赏，无赦罚〔72〕

An enlightened sovereign should neither grant rewards at will, nor absolve culprits from punishment without reason.

明君无为于上，群臣竦惧乎下〔74〕

If an enlightened sovereign governs through inaction, then his ministers will be circumspect in their deeds.

明君之道，臣不得陈言而不当〔76〕

The way to become an enlightened sovereign is to request that no minister speaks irresponsible words.

明君之所以立功成名者四〔78〕

To become an enlightened sovereign, one requires four prerequisites.

明君之行赏也，暖乎如时雨〔80〕

When an enlightened sovereign bestows rewards, they will benefit all, like a falling rain in a time of drought.

明君之于内也，娱其色而不行其谒〔82〕

An enlightened sovereign should appreciate the beauty of his wife and concubines yet not take heed of their gossip ...

明主使其群臣不游意于法之外〔84〕

An intelligent sovereign will not allow his ministers to gain privileges above the law ...

明主者，不恃其不我叛也〔86〕

An intelligent sovereign will not expect others to be faithful to him ...

明主之为官职爵禄也〔88〕

An intelligent sovereign will create positions and rewards in order to choose talented people and encourage those of merit.

明主之治国也，明赏，则民劝功〔90〕

An intelligent sovereign governs a country by bestowing liberal rewards for good conduct ...

母欺子，子而不信其母〔92〕

If a mother cheats her child, her child will no longer have trust in her.

目不明，则不能决黑白之分〔94〕

Without the aid of keen eyes we can not distinguish black from white.

目失镜，则无以正须眉〔96〕

We cannot groom our beards and brows without a mirror ...

N

能有其国、保其身者，必且体道〔98〕

A person who can protect his country and himself will act in accordance with the basic principles.

Q

千钧得船则浮，锱铢失船则沉〔100〕

An object as heavy as a thousand kilograms can float on the water's surface with the help of a boat; yet without a boat, smaller things will sink into the water.

千丈之堤，以蝼蚁之穴溃〔102〕

A dike of a thousand li can be destroyed by a single ant hole.

去好去恶，臣乃见素〔104〕

If the emperor does not reveal his preferences and dislikes, his ministers will reveal their true colors.

权不欲见，素无为也〔106〕

The emperor should take a humble attitude to his power and not flaunt it wantonly.

R

人主不合参验而行诛〔108〕

If a sovereign kills a man without investigation . . .

人主者，非目若离娄乃为明也〔110〕

A sovereign does not have to possess such sharp eyes as those of Li Lou's in order to be enlightened . . .

人主之道，静退以为宝〔112〕

A sovereign's guiding principle of conduct must be to constantly remain self-possessed and humble.

人主之患在莫之应〔114〕

The anxiety of an emperor stems from an absence of response

from his ministers, as he who stands alone has no power.

仁者，谓其中心欣然爱人也〔116〕

A benevolent person loves other people.

日月晕围于外，其贼在内〔118〕

Though solar and lunar halos surround the periphery of the sun and the moon, they are formed from within them.

S

善任势者国安，不知因其势者国危〔120〕

When a sovereign is skilful in holding his power, the country will be safe. When a sovereign is weak in maintaining his power, the country will be in danger.

赏莫如厚，使民利之〔122〕

Rewards should not be otherwise than liberal, so that people will consider them beneficial.

赏无功之人，罚不辜之民，非所谓明也〔124〕

It is unwise to reward men of no merit and to punish the innocent.

上有所长，事乃不方〔126〕

If a sovereign always flaunts his talents, his ministers will be weak in handling their affairs.

绳直而枉木斫，准夷而高科削〔128〕

If the inked string is straight, crooked timbers will be shaved; if the water-level is even, high gnarls will be planed down.

圣人衣足以犯寒，食足以充虚〔130〕

The saintly men, if they have sufficient clothes to resist the cold and sufficient food to fill their empty stomachs ...

圣人执一以静〔132〕

The enlightened sovereign remains in tranquility ...

圣人执要，四方来效〔134〕

If the emperor holds his power firmly, officials from all directions will come to render him service.

圣人之道，去智与巧〔136〕

The way of an enlightened sovereign is to discard his scheming and tricks.

市之无虎也明矣，然而三人言而成虎〔138〕

It may be clear that there is no tiger in the market ...

事以密成，语以泄败〔140〕

Affairs can succeed if they are kept secret, yet fail if they are divulged.

数披其木，毋使枝大本小〔142〕

The branches of a tree should be trimmed often to avoid them growing larger than the trunk from which they stem.

树橘柚者，食之则甘，嗅之则香〔144〕

The planter of orange and pomelo trees, upon eating and smelling the fruits obtains their sweet taste ...

水之胜火亦明矣，然而釜鬵间之〔146〕

It is clear that water can overpower fire. Yet, when a pot comes between them ...

虽无飞，飞必冲天〔148〕

Though it has not flown for three years, once it starts flying it will soar high into the sky.

所说出于为名高者也，而说之以厚利〔150〕

If a person strives for fame while the advisor persuades him to pursue profit ...

所说出于厚利者也，而说之以名高〔152〕

If a person strives for profit while the advisor persuades him to work for fame ...

T

太山之功长立于国家〔154〕

Only with the support of his people, an emperor's great achievements can stand eternally, like Mt. Tai.

天下有信数三〔156〕

There are three truths under heaven ...

W

外举不避仇，内举不避亲〔158〕

Recommend the right man who is competent, be he your family or your enemy.

X

惜草茅者耗禾穗，惠盗贼者伤良民〔160〕

Whoever spares the weeds, hurts the crops; whoever tolerates thieves and robbers, injures good citizens.

香美脆味，厚酒肥肉，甘口而疾形〔162〕

Rich food and good wine are delicious to the palate, but they can damage the body.

削株无遗根，无与祸邻〔164〕

If you leave no root when cutting down a tree, and be no neighbor to disaster ...

刑当无多，不当无少〔166〕

Punishments for crimes are not appraised by quantity, but by their equivalence.

刑过不避大臣，赏善不遗匹夫〔168〕

Punishments for crimes should never exclude ministers; rewards for merit should never pass over commoners.

刑胜而民静，赏繁而奸生〔170〕

If penalties are strict, the people will keep public order; if rewards are too easily attained, wickedness will appear in society.

虚静以待，令名自命也，令事自定也〔172〕

Resting in emptiness and repose, the emperor manages everything so that all terms will define themselves and all affairs will be settled in themselves.

Y

言赏则不与，言罚则不行〔174〕

If neither rewards are bestowed as promised nor punishments carried out as sworn ...

以乱攻治者亡，以邪攻正者亡〔176〕

Failure is assured if a misgoverned country attacks a well-governed country; if a wicked country attacks a righteous country ...

以尊主御忠臣，则长乐生而功名成〔178〕

When a noble sovereign governs loyal ministers, a country's long-term peace and stability can be maintained and thus its success and good reputation can be achieved.

因可势，求易道〔180〕

When dealing with affairs, one should seek favorable circumstances and the easiest path to success...

用一之道，以名为首，名正物定〔182〕

The way to govern a country begins with identifying the name in which to govern the country. When in the right name, the nature of things will become clear.

有材而无势，虽贤不能制不肖〔184〕

Without power and influence, even a talented sage cannot subdue the treacherous.

有赏者君见其功，有罚者君知其罪〔186〕

Of the rewarded, the emperor knows the meritorious service they rendered; of the punished, the emperor knows the criminal offence they committed.

舆人成舆，则欲人之富贵〔188〕

When a cartwright finishes making carriages, he wants people to be rich and noble.

Z

智士者远见而畏于死亡，必不从重人矣〔190〕

The wise men, far-sighted and afraid of death, will never commit crimes out of obedience to high-ranking ministers.

智术之士，必远见而明察〔192〕

Men who are acquainted with the principles of governing a country are always prescient and clear-sighted.

智术能法之士用〔194〕

If people who know how to govern a country and those who can uphold the law are appointed to governing posts . . .

众人多而圣人寡〔196〕

The masses are many, the saintly men are few.

主道者，使人臣有必言之责〔198〕

The right way to be a sovereign is to make all ministers hold the personal responsibility for either giving their opinions . . .

主利在有能而任官〔200〕

The sovereign can benefit from appointing able men to office . . .

韩非子说
HAN FEI ZI SAYS

　　韩非,战国末期杰出思想家,先秦法家集大成者。韩国贵族,喜刑名法术之学,也善于吸收儒家、道家、墨家、名家的一些思想,形成自己臻于完善的法家思想体系。韩非为人口吃,不善言辞,而善著书。与秦廷尉李斯同为荀子学生,斯自以为不如非。韩非见韩国势弱,数次上书谏韩王变法图强,韩王不用。愤世嫉俗的韩非看到当时"儒者以文乱法,而侠者以武犯禁"的现实,于是埋头著书,写了《孤愤》、《五蠹》、《内外储》、《说难》等篇,十余万言,后人辑为《韩非子》一书。

　　当时踌躇满志的秦始皇正在作统一中国的战争布局,偶见《孤愤》、《五蠹》两篇文章,以为先贤所作,感叹不已。后知其为韩国公子,于是下令急攻韩国,韩王危急时刻派韩非子使秦,秦始皇得到韩非后却没有重用,李斯乘机将他害死狱中。

Han Fei was a great Chinese philosopher and formulator of Legalism during the end of the Warring States

Period (475 – 221 BC) and up until the pre-Qin era. Born into an aristocratic royal family of the State of Han, he was always interested in the studies of jurisprudence and legal techniques. He also assimilated thoughts from Confucianism, Taoism, Mohism and Logician to form his complete ideology of Legalism. Although Han Fei stuttered and was slow to speak, he was sharp and insightful in his writings. Han Fei saw the decline of the state of Han and tried on several occasions to write to the king to propose different policies, but the king would not follow his advice. Seeing that in the chaotic society of the day, philosophers challenged the laws through their works and knights contravened them through their acts of daring, the resentful Han Fei buried himself in writing books such as *Solitary Indignation* (*Gu Fen*), *Five Vermin* (*Wu Du*), *Precautions Within the Palace* (*Nei Wai Chu*) and *Difficulties of Persuasion* (*Shui Nan*) among others. Over his lifetime he wrote many works which were later collected into a book named *Han Fei Zi*.

It was just as the ambitious King of Qin, future first Emperor of China, was planning to fight a war to unite the whole nation that he came across the two books *Solitary Indignation* and *Five Vermin*. He was deeply impressed by them, believing them to have been written by renowned scholars of older generation. When he learned that these works had been written by Han Fei, he ordered a sudden attack on the State of Han. During the crisis the King of the State of Han sent Han Fei as an envoy to Qin.

Yet the King of Qin did not trust Han Fei with any important position, and in the end he was imprisoned and eventually killed after Han Fei's former classmate, Li Si, made false claims against him to the King of Qin.

爱弃发之费而忘长发之利

People who, when washing their hair, regret the loss of the hairs that fall and forget the gain of the hairs that grow . . .

爱弃发之费而忘长发之利，不知权者也。

《韩非子·六反》

People who, when washing their hair, regret the loss of the hairs that fall and forget the gain of the hairs that grow, do not know the principle of observing the advantages and disadvantages of a situation.

【注释】

"六反"就是六种奸伪之民，本应受到斥责反而得到称誉；六种耕战之民，本应得到称誉反而受到斥责。韩非子强调，不能把错误的社会舆论作为赏罚的依据。他引用古人谚语说："法治好比洗头发一样，即使会有一些头发掉落，但洗头发还是必须的。"因为不能只看重掉头发的损耗，而忘记了促使头发生长的好处。

【译文】

（洗头发）只看重掉头发的损耗，而忘记促使头发生长的好处，这是不懂得权衡利弊的人。

不以小功妨大务

Agricultural cultivation should not be obstructed by trifles.

韩非子说

不以小功妨大务，不以私欲害人事。

《韩非子·难二》

Agricultural cultivation should not be obstructed by trifles; farming and weaving should not be hindered by selfish desires.

【注释】

李克治理中山时，因怀疑苦陉县令虚报产量而要罢免他。韩非子认为农耕顺应自然变化，种植根据四季作合理安排，不误农时。不因小事妨碍农耕，不因私欲妨害耕织，男子尽力农耕，女子致力纺织，收入就会多。并不一定报收入多就是虚报，除非你掌握了别人弄虚作假的证据。**小功**：小事。功，劳绩。《周礼·夏官》："王功曰勋，国功曰功。" **大务**：大事，指农耕。《史记·文帝纪》："农，天下之本，务莫大焉。" **人事**：人力所能及的事。此处指耕织之事。

【译文】

不因小事妨碍农耕，不因私欲妨害耕织。

豺狼在牢，其羊不繁。

If wolves get into a sheepfold, the sheep will not flourish.

豺狼在牢，其羊不繁。一家二贵，事乃无功。夫妻持政，子无适从。

《韩非子·扬权》

If wolves get into a sheepfold, the sheep will not flourish. If imperious ministers come into power, the country will not prosper. If two people try to make the decisions in a family, the family will not be well-managed. If a married couple both attempt to govern their household, their children will not know whom to obey.

【注释】

豺狼在牢，其羊不繁：豺狼入圈，羊不蕃息。牢，关养牲畜的栏圈。《诗经·大雅·公刘》："执豕于牢，酌之用匏。"韩非子的意思是说，权臣当政，国家不能繁荣。贵：位尊。《易·系辞上》："卑高以陈，贵贱位矣。"

【译文】

豺狼入圈，羊不繁殖；权臣当政，国不繁荣。一家两个主管，家治理不好；夫妻同时当家，子女无所适从。

诚有功，则虽疏贱必赏

Rewards should be given to those of real merit, even if they are distant and humble.

诚有功，则虽疏贱必赏；诚有过，则虽近爱必诛。疏贱必赏，近爱必诛，则疏贱者不怠，而近爱者不骄也。

《韩非子·主道》

Rewards should be given to those of real merit, even if they are distant and humble. Punishments should be meted out to those without scruples, even if they are near and beloved. If both rewards and punishments are bestowed infallibly, the distant and humble will not become idle and the near and beloved will develop self-discipline.

【注释】

韩非子说："明君不会随便赏赐，也不会无故赦免刑罚。赏赐随便了，功臣就会懈怠于他的职务；刑罚无故被赦免了，奸臣就会变本加厉为非歹。"诚：果然，确实。《孟子·公孙丑上》："子诚齐人也，知管仲晏子而已矣。"诛：惩罚。

【译文】

对确实有功的人，即使是关系疏远、地位卑贱的人也一定赏赐；对确实有罪的人，即使是亲近喜爱的人也一定要惩罚。疏远卑贱的人必赏，亲近喜爱的人必罚，那么疏远卑贱的人就不会懈怠，而亲近喜爱的人就不会骄横了。

聪明睿智，天也

The hearing, sight and intelligence of man are endowed by nature.

老人家说系列丛书

聪明睿智，天也；动静思虑，人
也。人也者，乘于天明以视，寄于天
聪以听，托于天智以思虑。

《韩非子·解老》

The hearing, sight and intelligence of man are endowed
by nature. Listening, seeing, and thinking are enacted by
man. Man, by virtue of hearing hears; by virtue of natural
sight sees; and thinks owing to natural intelligence, in order
to gain material comforts.

【注释】

聪：听觉，听觉好。天聪：犹言天听，天赋的听觉。明：视觉，视觉好。天明：
天赋的视觉。睿（ruì）：聪明。天智：天赋的智慧。乘（chéng）：利用，趁机会。
《韩非子·八经·起乱》："故明主审公私之分，审利害之地，奸乃无所乘。"寄：依
附。托：依托。《战国策·赵策四》："一旦山陵崩，长安君何以自托于赵？"

【译文】

人的听力、视力和智力是天然生成的，用它们去
听、去看、去思虑则是人为的。人为了获得物质享受，
依靠天赋的听觉去听，依靠天赋的视觉去看，依靠天赋
的智慧去思虑。

大不可量，深不可测

The emperor's governing skill is too great to be measured and too profound to be surveyed.

韩非子说

大不可量，深不可测，同合刑名，审验法式，擅为者诛，国乃无贼。

《韩非子·主道》

The emperor's governing skill is too great to be measured and too profound to be surveyed. He must determine if the words and deeds of the ministers are in accord, scrutinize whether they abide by the laws and chastise those who don't. As a result there will be no treacherous people within the country.

【注释】

刑：通"形"，行为的表现。法式：法度，法则。《荀子·礼论》："大象其生以送其死，使死生终始莫不称宜而好善，是礼义之法式也。"擅（shàn）：独断专行。《韩非子·孤愤》："当涂之人擅事要，则外内为之用矣。"

【译文】

君主的治术大到不可估量，深到不可探测，考核臣下言行是否一致，考察臣下活动是否合于法度，严惩擅自妄为的人，国家就没有奸贼了。

大费无罪而少得为功

If those who waste large sums of money receive no punishment and those who make small achievements are rewarded . . .

大费无罪而少得为功，则人臣出大费而成小功，小功成而主亦有害。

《韩非子·南面》

If those who waste large sums of money receive no punishment and those who make small achievements are rewarded, ministers will spend large sums of money to make small achievements. Although small achievements are attained, in the end the country will suffer losses.

【注释】

韩非子说："做事的原则应该是利益多、代价小的就可以做。昏君就不是这样，只看得利，不计代价，代价即使大过利益数倍也去做，而不知它的危害，这名义上是获利，实际上则是受害。大凡功劳，应该是代价小而获利多。现在耗费多无罪，而收效小却有功，如此臣子就会不计成本大、投入多而贪求小利，虽然取得了小利，而君主仍是遭到了损害。"

【译文】

耗费大的无罪，收效小的却有功，臣子就会以大的耗费去换取小的成效。小的成效虽然取得了，而国家实际上受到了损害。

耽于女乐，不顾国政

A country's downfall begins if the emperor indulges in carnal pleasures and neglects state affairs.

耽于女乐，不顾国政，则亡国之祸也。

《韩非子·十过》

A country's downfall begins if the emperor indulges in carnal pleasures and neglects state affairs.

【注释】

韩非子认为君主、大臣有十种过错足以造成亡身、亡国之祸。"女乐亡国"就是十过之一。秦穆公为削弱西戎国，便送去女歌舞乐队，以迷惑其国君，同时离间其君臣关系。西戎国君得女乐队，沉湎声色，不事国政，致"终岁不迁，牛马半死"。终因国势衰弱，被秦国占领。耽（dān）：沉溺，入迷。女乐：歌舞伎。《左传·襄公十一年》："郑人赂晋侯以师悝……女乐二八。"注："十六人。"

【译文】

（君主）沉溺于女乐，不顾国家政事，就会招来亡国之祸。

道譬诸若水，溺者多饮之即死

Tao can be compared to water. The drowned die from drinking too much . . .

道譬诸若水，溺者多饮之即死，渴者适饮之即生；譬之若剑戟，愚人以行忿则祸生，圣人以诛暴则福成。

《韩非子·解老》

Tao can be compared to water. The drowned die from drinking too much, while the thirsty survive by drinking in moderation. Tao can also be compared to swords and halberds. If the stupid man uses it for wreaking his vengeance upon others, disaster will befall him. If the saintly man uses it for punishing the wrong, good luck will be bestowed upon the people.

【注释】

韩非子说："凡属道的真情，不做作，不外露，柔弱和顺，随时运行，与理相应。万物因得道而死亡，因得道而生存；万事因得道而失败，因得道而成功。如果把道比喻成水，溺水者喝多了就会死，口渴的人适量饮用就能生存。再把道比喻成剑和戟，愚人拿来行凶泄愤就会惹祸，圣人拿来诛杀残暴就能造福。所以说，因得道而死，因得道而生；因得道而失败，因得道而成功。按照事物的法则办事的人，没有不成功的。"

【译文】

如果把道比喻成水，溺水者喝多了就会淹死，口渴的人适量饮用就能生存。再把道比喻成剑和戟，愚人拿来行凶泄愤就会惹祸，圣人拿来诛杀残暴就能为民造福。

道在不可见，用在不可知

Tao is invisible, thus no one knows when the emperor employs it.

道在不可见，用在不可知。虚静无事，以暗见疵。

《韩非子·主道》

Tao is invisible, thus no one knows when the emperor employs it. Therefore, the emperor should always remain serene to be able to observe discreetly the errors of his ministers.

【注释】

道：指君主掌握的道。实际上这里说的道是指君主驾驭臣下的"术"。韩非子的政治思想主要由商鞅的法、申不害的术和慎到的势三部分组成。疵（cī）：小毛病。引申为过失，缺点。《易·系辞上》："悔吝者，言乎其小疵也。"

【译文】

道是看不见的，君主运用道的时候，也不能被察觉。君主要保持虚静无事的态度，以隐蔽的方法察看群臣的过失。

道者，万物之始，是非之纪也

Tao is the beginning point of all lives and the source of right and wrong.

道者，万物之始，是非之纪也。是以明君守始以知万物之源，治纪以知善败之端。

《韩非子·主道》

As Tao is the beginning point of all lives and the source of right and wrong, the enlightened sovereign can use Tao to understand the origins of nature and comprehend the causes of success and failure.

【注释】

韩非子把道家虚静无为的哲学思想运用到政治生活中，发展成为君主治国用人的原则，故称"主道"。纪：法度，准则。《吕氏春秋·孟春》："无变天之道，无绝地之理，无乱人之纪。"守始：把握住"道"。守，保持。《易·系辞下》："圣人之大宝曰位，何以守位曰仁。"始，开端，最初，指"道"。《老子》第1章："无名，天地之始；有名，万物之母。"治纪：研究准则。治，管理，疏理。《论语·宪问》："王孙贾治军旅。"善败：成败。《左传·僖公二十年》："量力而动，其过鲜矣；善败由己，而由人乎哉？"端：开头，引申为缘由。

【译文】

道是万物的本原、是非的准则。因此英明的君主把握住"道"来了解万物的起源，研究事物准则来了解成败的原因。

得天时，则不多而自生

At the right time, the crops will flourish without great effort.

得天时，则不务而自生；得人心，则不趣而自劝。

《韩非子·功名》

At the right time, the crops will flourish without great effort. With the support of the people, the emperor can rule the country without undue force, as his people will be willing to cultivate themselves.

【注释】

韩非子说："不顺天时，即使有十个尧帝也不能让庄稼在冬天扬花抽穗；违背了民意，即使孟贲、夏育这样的勇士也不能让老百姓出力气。"孟贲、夏育：战国时卫国著名勇士。**趣**（cù）：古同"促"。督促。《礼记·月令》"季秋之月"一部分文字中有"乃趣狱刑，毋留有罪"的句子。**劝**：勉励。

【译文】

顺应天时，即使不费力，庄稼也会自然生长；顺应民心，不用督促，老百姓也会自我勉励。

德也者，人之所以建生也

Morality is the root of existence.

德也者，人之所以建生也；禄也者，人之所以持生也。今建于理者，其持禄也久。

《韩非子·解老》

Morality is the root of existence, and wealth generated by one's position ensures his living. If a person's morality is grounded upon reason, then he can keep his position for a very long time.

【注释】

韩非子曰："树木有曼根，有直根。直根者，书之所谓'柢'也。柢也者，木之所以建生也；曼根者，木之所以持生也。"建生：生长的支柱。建，直立。《尚书·大传·略说》："九十杖而朝，见君建杖。"禄：俸禄，官吏的俸给。《礼记·王制》："位定，然后禄之。"注："与之以常食。"持生：扶助生长。持，扶助。理：道理，法则。《易·系辞上》："易简而天下之理得矣。"

【译文】

德是人立身为人的根本，俸禄是人维持生计的保障。如今的人若能立身守则，那么他的官位就能做得长久。

罚薄不为慈，诛严不为戾

It is not an act of charity to administer light penalties, nor is it an act of cruelty to enforce strict ones.

罚薄不为慈，诛严不为戾，称俗而行也。

《韩非子·五蠹》

It is not an act of charity to administer light penalties, nor is it an act of cruelty to enforce strict ones. Penalties should be meted out in accordance with the social order of the age.

【注释】

"五蠹"是韩非子法治思想的代表作。蠹（dù）：蛀虫。韩非子把儒家、纵横家、游侠、逃避兵役的人和经营工商业者看成是破坏法治的蛀虫。戾（lì）：凶暴。称俗：适应世俗。称，相当，符合。《荀子·富国》："德必称位，位必称禄，禄必称用。"俗，习俗，风气。《尚书·君陈》："败常乱俗。"

【译文】

刑罚轻不是仁慈，责罚严不是凶暴，是适应社会情况而行事。

法败则国乱，民怨则国危

If laws are not obeyed, the country will be in chaos. If the people exist in hatred, the country will be in danger.

法败则国乱，民怨则国危。

《韩非子·难一》

If laws are not obeyed, the country will be in chaos. If the people exist in hatred, the country will be in danger.

【注释】

晋、齐交战，晋中军司马韩厥将斩人，主帅郤克听说后，驾车赶去救人。等他赶到时，人已处死。郤克说："为什么不把他的尸体巡行示众？"郤克的侍仆说："您不是要救他吗？为什么又这样说？"郤克说："我怎敢不为韩厥分担别人对他的非议呢？"韩非子认为法不赦罪人，不杀无辜。如果韩厥所斩是有罪的人，郤克就不该去救。救有罪的人会致法纪败坏，国家就混乱。如果所斩不是罪人，郤克就不应再让韩厥将尸体巡行示众，无辜的人被杀尸体又被示众，会使民众产生怨恨，民众怨恨，国家就危险。

【译文】

法纪败坏，国家就会混乱；民众怨恨，国家就有危险。

法不阿贵，绳不挠曲

Laws do not favor the ministers in power, just as an ink marker does not make a curved line on its own.

法不阿贵，绳不挠曲。

《韩非子·有度》

Laws do not favor the ministers in power, just as an ink marker does not make a curved line on its own.

【注释】

韩非子曰："法之所加，智者弗能辞，勇者弗敢争。"**阿**（ē）：曲从，迎合。《国语·吴语》："勾践愿诸大夫言之，皆以情告，无阿孤。"《吕氏春秋·达郁》："侍者为吾听行于齐王也，夫何阿哉?"**挠**（náo）：屈服。《战国策·魏策四》："（唐且）挺剑而起，秦王色挠，长跪而谢之。"引申为迁就。

【译文】

法令不偏袒权贵，墨线不迁就弯曲。

法莫如显，而术不欲见

Laws should be made clear and public, while the methods of ruling the subordinates should be kept hidden.

法莫如显，而术不欲见。

《韩非子·难三》

Laws should be made clear and public, while the methods of ruling the subordinates should be kept hidden.

【注释】

韩非子认为，法之所以要公开发布，是为了让天下人都知道，都能遵照执行，国家才能大治。术是君主用来驾驭臣下的机密，所以要深藏不露。"术者，藏之于胸中，以偶众端而潜御群臣者也"。

【译文】

法令越公开越好，驾驭群臣的办法却不能显露出来。

夫虎之所以能服狗者，爪牙也

A tiger can overcome a dog by virtue of its claws and teeth.

夫虎之所以能服狗者，爪牙也；使虎释其爪牙而使狗用之，则虎反服于狗矣。

《韩非子·二柄》

A tiger can overcome a dog by virtue of its claws and teeth. However, if the tiger lost its claws and teeth to the dog, then it would be subservient to the dog's power.

【注释】

韩非子曰："人主者，以刑、德制臣者也，今君人者释其刑、德而使臣用之，则君反制于臣矣。""二柄"指刑与德，即惩罚与奖赏两种权柄。这里以虎靠爪牙制狗为喻。**爪牙**：爪和牙，鸟兽用于攻击和防卫。《荀子·劝学》："蚓无爪牙之利，筋骨之强。"**释**：去掉。

【译文】

老虎能制服狗，靠的是爪和牙；如果老虎把爪牙让给狗使用，那老虎反而会受制于狗。

夫使民有功与无功俱赏者

If both people of merit and demerit are equally rewarded . . .

夫使民有功与无功俱赏者，此乱之道也。

《韩非子·外储说右下》

If both people of merit and demerit are equally rewarded, the state will be in disorder.

【注释】

秦国遭遇饥荒，应侯请求秦王开放五处苑场，让百姓进内取食菜蔬果实以度荒。秦王说："秦国的法令是有功受赏，有罪受罚。如果开放苑场让百姓进去取食，是有功无功俱受赏，那是使国家混乱的做法。"韩非子所讲"有功受赏，有罪受罚"的原则是对的，但秦王把救灾和无功受赏混为一谈却有违法治的本质。所以司马迁说法家"苛薄寡恩"。

【译文】

不论有功无功都受赏赐，这是使国家混乱的做法。

夫物者有所宜，材者有所施

Just as all things have different functions, all people are endowed with special talents.

夫物者有所宜，材者有所施，各处其宜，故上下无为。使鸡司夜，令狸执鼠，皆用其能，上乃无事。

《韩非子·扬权》

Just as all things have different functions, all people are endowed with special talents. When everything is put to proper use and people are appointed to appropriate positions, the sovereign can enjoy stability and be at peace. Just as the rooster crows at daybreak, and the cat hunts the mouse, everyone and everything shall be well ordered and the sovereign will be without worry.

【注释】

韩非子认为君主居高无上，但并非独揽一切权力、独断专行，而是"事在四方，要在中央"。四方官员各尽其责，中央集权才能巩固。**宜**：合适，相称。《荀子·正名》："名无固宜，约之以命。约定俗成谓之宜，异于约则谓之不宜。"**材**：才能，才干。通"才"。《尚书·咸有一德》："任官惟贤材，左右惟其人。"**司**：主管。**狸**：猫，古代称猫为狸。

【译文】

事物各有特性，人各有所长，使其各处其位，君主就能清静无为。犹如让鸡司晨，让猫捕鼠，各司其职，各尽其能，国君才能清静无事。

凡治天下，必因人情

When governing a country, the ruler should take worldly wisdom into consideration.

老人家说系列丛书

凡治天下，必因人情。人情者有好恶，故赏罚可用；赏罚可用，则禁令可立，而治道具矣。

《韩非子·八经》

When governing a country, the ruler should take worldly wisdom into consideration. People will always try to seek out advantages and avoid disadvantages, thus rewards and punishments will always be able to be employed in governing. When rewards and punishments are employed, orders can be enforced, and a solid system of rule can be created.

【注释】

韩非子认为，赏罚是否可行，不是由君主的意志决定的，而应由人情来决定。人有趋利避害之性，赏罚才有实行的可能。人不受赏、不畏罚，赏罚就失去了作用。**人情**：人之常情。《庄子·逍遥游》："大有径庭，不近人情焉。"

【译文】

凡要治理天下，必须依人情行事。人有趋利避害之性，因而赏罚可以使用，法令就可以建立起来，治国的政策也就能完备起来。

功当其事，事当其言，则赏

Ministers whose accomplishments equal their words should be rewarded.

功当其事，事当其言，则赏；功不当其事，事不当其言，则罚。

《韩非子·二柄》

Ministers whose accomplishments equal their words should be rewarded; if their accomplishments do not equal their words they should be punished.

【注释】

韩非子说：君主正确掌握赏罚之权，必须"审合刑名"，即审察臣下的言论与事功是否相符，相符则赏，不相符则罚。"故群臣其言大而功小者则罚，非罚小功也，罚功不当名也。群臣其言小而功大者亦罚，非不说于大功也，以为不当名也，害甚于有大功，故罚。"

【译文】

对臣下言论与事功相符者，则赏赐；不相符者，则惩罚。

工匠不得施其技巧，故屋坏弓折

If artisans are not able to utilize their skills, houses will fall and bows will break.

工匠不得施其技巧，故屋坏弓折；知治之人不得行其方术，故国乱而主危。

《韩非子·外储说左上》

If artisans are not able to utilize their skills, houses will fall and bows will break. If people with the talent to govern are not valued, the country will be in disorder and the sovereign will be in danger.

【注释】

赵人虞卿造屋时自以为是，不听工匠的话，结果房子倒塌了。魏人范雎造弓时不听工匠的话，最后弓折断了。韩非子认为范雎、虞卿的说法似乎很有道理，但却违背了实际情况，所以君主不谋求治国强兵的实际功效，却欣赏那些动听的诡辩之辞，这实际上是排斥有治国方法的思想，而采纳那些导致屋塌、弓折的胡说。

【译文】

工匠不能施展技巧，所以会有房倒、弓折的结果；懂得治国方法的人不被重视，所以国家混乱，君主处境危险。

火形严，故人鲜灼

As fire seems frightening, people escape from it and seldom are burned.

火形严，故人鲜灼；水形懦，人多溺。

《韩非子·内储说上》

As fire seems frightening, people escape from it and seldom are burned; as water seems mild, people feel drawn to it and often are drowned.

【注释】

　　子产做郑相，重病将死，对其子游吉说："我死之后，你一定会在郑国执政，一定要依法治民，从严执行刑罚。火的样子是严酷的，人们避之唯恐不及，所以人们很少被烧伤；水的样子是柔和的，人们乐于接近，所以很多人被淹死。"子产死后，游吉不肯从严执法，郑国青年中很多人拉帮结伙成为强盗，以身试法，结果给郑国造成很大的祸害。鲜（xiǎn）：少。灼（zhuó）：烧伤。

【译文】

　　火的样子是严酷的，人们避之唯恐不及，所以人们很少被烧伤；水的样子是柔和的，人们乐于接近，所以很多人被淹死。

祸难生于邪心，邪心诱于可欲

Disasters grow out of evil thoughts. Evil thoughts are induced by greed.

祸难生于邪心，邪心诱于可欲。可欲之类，进则教良民为奸，退则令善人有祸。

《韩非子·解老》

Disasters grow out of evil thoughts. Evil thoughts are induced by greed. Greed may cause good citizens to be wicked and bring kind persons calamity.

【注释】

韩非子曰："人有欲，则计会乱；计会乱，而有欲甚；有欲甚，则邪心胜；邪心胜，则事经绝；事经绝，则祸难生。" **邪**：不正。《尚书·大禹谟》："任贤勿贰，去邪勿疑。"

【译文】

灾难产生于邪心，邪心产生于欲望。可引起贪欲的东西，进可以使好人为奸，退可以使善人遭殃。

今欲以先王之政，治当世之民

If we adhere to the ruling system of previous kings to govern the current people . . .

今欲以先王之政，治当世之民，皆守株之类也。

《韩非子·五蠹》

If we adhere to the ruling system of previous kings to govern the current people, we are acting like the fool who waits by the tree for a rabbit to appear.

【注释】

韩非子以"守株待兔"的寓言故事，比喻守旧者的愚蠢可笑。他所说的守旧人物首先指死守旧制度并用旧办法治理国家的君主大臣，他们只会拘泥旧制、抱残守缺而不去探寻变法图强的道路。韩非子讥讽这些人不过是愚不可及的"守株者"。先王：指尧、舜、禹、汤和周文王、周武王。

【译文】

现在假如还要用先王之政来治理当代的百姓，那无疑和守株待兔的蠢人一样可笑。

禁奸之法，太上禁其心

Among the methods of suppressing evil deeds, the best is to curb a wicked mind.

禁奸之法，太上禁其心，其次禁其言，其次禁其事。

《韩非子·说疑》

Among the methods of suppressing evil deeds, the best is to curb a wicked mind, the next, the villainous words, and the last, vicious actions.

【注释】

韩非子认为，治国大事不仅是赏罚。赏无功罚无罪，不能算明察。就是完全做到赏有功，罚有罪，也不能从根本上起到建功止过的效果，因此禁止奸邪的首要问题是禁止产生奸邪的思想，然后才是禁止奸邪的言论和行为。太上：最上，最重要的，最好的。《老子》第17章："太上，不知有之；其次，亲而誉之；其次，畏之；其次，侮之。"心：指思考。《易·系辞上》："二人同心，其利断金。"

【译文】

禁止奸邪的首要问题，在于首先禁止产生奸邪的思想，其次是禁止奸邪的言论，最后才是禁止奸邪的行为。

镜无见疵之罪，道无明过之怨

As mirror should not be punished due to its reflection of flaws, Tao should not be hated because of its exposure of wrong doings.

韩非子说

镜无见疵之罪，道无明过之怨。

《韩非子·观行》

As mirror should not be punished due to its reflection of flaws, Tao should not be hated because of its exposure of wrong doings.

【注释】

"观行"就是观察自己和他人的行为。韩非子认为，人的智慧和才能各有其局限，英明的君主要知道自己的长处和短处。他说："古代的人因为知道眼睛缺少自见的能力，所以发明镜子来观察自己的面容；因为知道智慧缺少自知的能力，所以用道来端正自己。所以，镜子不应承受显现瑕疵的罪责，道不应承受显露过失的怨恨。"疵（cī）：小病。引申为过失、缺点。晋赵孟因其脸上有疵点，故绰号"疵面"。

【译文】

镜子不应承受显现瑕疵的罪责，道不应承受显露过失的怨恨。

君无见其所欲

The sovereign should not expose his preferences.

君无见其所欲，君见其所欲，臣自将雕琢；君无见其意，君见其意，臣将自表异。

《韩非子·主道》

The sovereign should not expose his preferences. If he does, his ministers may pretend to have the same inclinations, in the name of flattery. The sovereign should not show his will. If he does, his ministers may feign to have the same designs.

【注释】

见：同"现"（xiàn）。显露。《论语·泰伯》："天下有道则见，无道则隐。"《战国策·燕策》："图穷而匕首见。"雕琢：修饰，矫正。《淮南子·精神》："直雕琢其性，矫拂其情，以与世交。"表异：伪装。陈奇猷《韩非子集释》案曰："表异，犹言表其异能也。"

【译文】

君主不可显露他的欲望，君主显露他的欲望，臣下就会为讨好君主而自我粉饰；君主不可显露他的意愿，君主显露他的意愿，臣下就会自我伪装。

君有道，则臣尽力而奸不生

If the sovereign adopts the right ruling system, his ministers will exert themselves to their utmost, and evil will not arise.

君有道，则臣尽力而奸不生；无道，则臣上塞主明而下成私。

《韩非子·难一》

If the sovereign adopts the right ruling system, his ministers will exert themselves to their utmost, and evil will not arise. If he does not adopt the right ruling system, his ministers will cheat him to gain secret profits.

【注释】

难（nàn）：有诘问、辩驳之意。管仲临终告诫齐桓公要除去竖刁、易牙等三个佞臣，而桓公不听，结果桓公重病时受到三个佞臣的陷害，饿死后不得安葬，以致尸腐出蛆。韩非子用辩难方式对此加以评说，他认为桓公的悲剧不是没有听管仲的告诫去除三个佞臣造成的，而是齐桓公没有用权势法术去驾驭臣下所致。

【译文】

君主有正确的治国原则，臣下就会尽力，奸邪就不会产生；君主没有正确的治国原则，臣下就会对上蒙蔽君主，在下谋取私利。

离朱易百步而难眉睫

Li Zhu could see a hair from a distance as far away as a hundred steps, yet not see his own eyebrows and lashes.

离朱易百步而难眉睫，非百步近
而眉睫远也，道不可也。

《韩非子·观行》

Li Zhu could see a hair from a distance as far away as a hundred steps, yet not see his own eyebrows and lashes. This is not because the hair was close to him and his brows and eyelashes were far, but because the situation did not permit such close self-inspection.

【注释】
韩非子曰："势有不可得，事有不可成。故乌获轻千钧而重其身，非其身重于千钧也，势不便也。离朱易百步而难眉睫，非百步近而眉睫远也，道不可也。故明主不穷乌获以其不能自举；不困离朱以其不能自见。"**离朱：**又作"离娄"，传为黄帝时人，视力极好，能轻易看清百步以外毫毛的尖端。**道：**条件。

【译文】
离朱能轻易看清百步之外的毫毛，却看不到自己的眉毛和睫毛，并非（因为）百步近而眉毛和睫毛远，是（因为）条件不允许。

吏者，民之本，纲者也
The officials are the roots of the people.

韩非子说

吏者，民之本，纲者也，故圣人治吏不治民。

《韩非子·外储说右下》

The officials are the roots of the people. Thus, a divine sovereign only needs to govern the officials, and not directly govern the people.

【注释】

摇动树干，整棵树上的叶子都会动起来；张网捕鱼的人只需纲举目张，而不用去逐一拨弄网眼就能网到鱼。官吏就像民众的"树干"和总纲，因此君主管理百姓只要管好官吏就行了。

【译文】

官吏就像民众的"树干"和总纲，因此圣明君主只需管理官吏而不用直接管理民众。

盲则不能避昼日之险

As a blind man cannot avoid danger in daylight ...

盲则不能避昼日之险，聋则不能知雷霆之害，狂则不能免人间法令之祸。

《韩非子·解老》

As a blind man cannot avoid danger in daylight, a deaf man cannot know the peril of thunder, and a morally unsound man cannot escape punishment for violating the law.

【注释】

韩非子曰："目不明，则不能决黑白之分；耳不聪，则不能别清浊之声；智识乱，则不能审得失之地。目不能决黑白之色则谓之盲，耳不能别清浊之声则谓之聋，心不能审得失之地则谓之狂。"狂：迷乱。《素问·宣明五气篇》："五邪所乱，邪入于阳则狂。"

【译文】

眼睛不明就不能躲避白天的危险，耳朵不灵就不能知道雷霆的危害，心智迷乱就不能免于社会法令的惩罚。

名实相持而成，形影相应而立

Names and reality depend upon each other; form and shadow are opposites.

名实相持而成，形影相应而立，故臣主同欲而异使。

《韩非子·功名》

Names and reality depend upon each other; form and shadow are opposites. Hence, the sovereign and the ministers, although having different missions, make the same wishes.

【注释】

名实：名称和实际。《管子·九守》"名实当则治，不当则乱。"《战国策·秦策一》："故拔一国而天下不以为暴；利尽西海，诸侯不以为贪，是我一举而名实两附。"

【译文】

名和实相互依赖而成立，形和影相互对应而出现，所以君臣愿望相同而各自的使命不一样。

明夫恃人不如自恃也

Everyone should understand that relying on oneself is better than relying upon others.

韩非子说

明夫恃人不如自恃也，明于人之为己者，不如己之自为也。

《韩非子·外储说右下》

Everyone should understand that relying on oneself is better than relying upon others, and that helping oneself is better than being helped by others.

【注释】

鲁相公仪休嗜鱼，全城的人争相买鱼进献给他，他却不收。显示了一位识大体、顾大局、有长远眼光的宰相的风范。他把个人嗜好同遵纪守法联系起来，认为他如果收了别人的鱼，就一定会迁就他们的过失而违背法令，违法就会被罢免相位，被免职后也就不会再有人给他送鱼了。

【译文】

懂得依靠别人不如依靠自己，知道靠别人帮助不如自己帮助自己的道理。

明君无偷赏，无赦罚

An enlightened sovereign should neither grant rewards at will, nor absolve culprits from punishment without reason.

明君无偷赏，无赦罚。赏偷，则功臣堕其业；赦罚，则奸臣易为非。

《韩非子·主道》

An enlightened sovereign should neither grant rewards at will, nor absolve culprits from punishment without reason. To grant rewards at will may cause the rewarded to be remiss in their duties and to absolve culprits from punishment without reason may encourage the fraudulent to become worse.

【注释】

偷赏：随便赏赐。偷，苟且，随便。《老子》第41章："建德若偷。"赦罚：赦免刑罚。赦，有罪而放免。《易·解》："君子以赦过宥罪。"堕（duò）：懈怠。通"惰"。《韩非子·显学》："与人相若也，无饥馑疾疚祸罪之殃，独以贫穷者，非侈则堕也。"

【译文】

明君不随便赏赐，不无故赦免刑罚。赏赐被随便给予了，功臣就会懈怠他的职事；刑罚被无故赦免了，奸臣就会变本加厉。

明君无为于上，群臣竦惧乎下

If an enlightened sovereign governs through inaction, then his ministers will be circumspect in their deeds.

明君无为于上，群臣竦惧乎下。

《韩非子·主道》

If an enlightened sovereign governs through inaction,
then his ministers will be circumspect in their deeds.

【注释】

韩非子曰："明君之道，使智者尽其虑，而君因以断事，故君不穷于智；贤者勑其材，君因而任之，故君不穷于能；有功则君有其贤，有过则臣任其罪，故君不穷于名。"无为：韩非子借用道家无为思想，把它用到治国理论之中，形成法家任势用术的最高原则。无为已经成为韩非子法制思想的理论基础。竦（sǒng）：通"悚"。害怕，恐惧。

【译文】

明君在上无为而治，群臣在下诚惶诚恐。

明君之道，臣不得陈言而不当

The way to become an enlightened sovereign is to request that no minister speaks irresponsible words.

明君之道，臣不得陈言而不当。

《韩非子·主道》

The way to become an enlightened sovereign is to request that no minister speaks irresponsible words.

【注释】

韩非子认为，君主是根据臣下陈述的主张而授予职事，然后根据职事考查臣下的办事功效，并由此决定赏罚，因此他要求臣下不能说话不负责任。陈言：陈述意见。《礼记·儒行》："儒有澡身而浴德，陈言而伏，静而正之。"当：担当，负责。

【译文】

英明君主的原则，要求臣下不能说不负责任的话。

明君之所以立功成名者四

To become an enlightened sovereign, one requires four prerequisites.

明君之所以立功成名者四：一曰天时，二曰人心，三曰技能，四曰势位。

《韩非子·功名》

To become an enlightened sovereign, one requires four prerequisites: first, rule at the right time; second, be supported by the people; third, use skills deftly; fourth, possess position and status.

【注释】

韩非子认为，君主要立功成名，必须具有四个条件：顺天时，得人心，运用技能和高居势位。顺应天时，五谷自然生长；得人心，民众就会自我勉励；凭借技能，事情就会办好；得到势位，就能名正言顺。好像水的流动、船的漂浮一样，掌握住自然法则，推行畅通无阻的法令，所以能称为明君。**势位**：势由位生，只有处于高位，才能握有权势。

【译文】

圣明君主立功成名有四个必备的条件：一是顺应天时，二是得人心，三是运用技能，四是高居势位。

明君之行赏也，暖乎如时雨

When an enlightened sovereign bestows rewards, they will benefit all, like a falling rain in a time of drought.

明君之行赏也，暧乎如时雨，百姓利其泽；其行罚也，畏乎如雷霆，神圣不解也。

《韩非子·主道》

When an enlightened sovereign bestows rewards, they will benefit all, like a falling rain in a time of drought; when he imposes punishments, they will affect even the sacred, like a terrifying thunderstorm.

【注释】

暧（ài）：浓云遮盖的样子。时雨：应时之雨。《国语·齐语》："时雨既至。" 神圣：指神灵。《素书·安礼》："非其神圣，自然所钟。"

【译文】

明君行赏，像应时之雨那样普降，老百姓都能受到他的恩泽；明君施罚，像雷霆那样可怕，就连神灵也不能解脱。

明君之于内也，娱其色而不行其谒

An enlightened sovereign should appreciate the beauty of his wife and concubines yet not take heed of their gossip . . .

明君之于内也，娱其色而不行其谒，不使私请。其于左右也，使其身必责其言，不使益辞。

《韩非子·八奸》

An enlightened sovereign should appreciate the beauty of his wife and concubines yet not take heed of their gossip, or answer their private requests. As to his attendants and servants, he should ask them to be cautious with their words and take care not to exaggerate.

【注释】

韩非子认为：八术，权臣用之，君辱国破；君主察之，国治主尊。八奸的形成，归根结底是君主不察，使权臣有机可乘所导致的，因此，防八奸应从君主自省自察不授人以柄做起。娱：欢乐，戏乐。谒：禀告，陈述。

【译文】

英明君主对待自己的夫人、宫妾，可以欣赏她们的美色但不要听她们的禀告，不准她们因私请求。对待身边的近侍，使用他们时一定要严察他们的言论，不准他们夸大其辞。

明主使其群臣不游意于法之外

An intelligent sovereign will not allow his ministers to gain privileges above the law . . .

明主使其群臣不游意于法之外，不为惠于法之内，动无非法。

《韩非子·有度》

An intelligent sovereign will not allow his ministers to gain privileges above the law, nor any private interests that are prohibited by the law. They must always follow the letter of the law.

【注释】

韩非子认为治国要有法度，有法度就是以法治国，故称"有度"。群臣既不能置身于法外，又不能在法内以权谋私。君主能否坚决推行法治，是决定国家强弱的关键。

【译文】

英明君主不会让他的臣下在法律之外拥有特权，也不允许他们在法令规定的范围内谋求私利，一举一动皆要遵纪守法。

明主者，不恃其不我叛也

An intelligent sovereign will not expect others to be faithful to him ...

明主者，不恃其不我叛也，恃吾不可叛也；不恃其不我欺也，恃吾不可欺也。

《韩非子·外储说左下》

An intelligent sovereign will not expect others to be faithful to him, but will instead inspire loyalty in his people. He will not rely upon others not deceiving him, but instead will be able to ensure honesty in his people.

【注释】

晋文公逃亡在外，箕郑带着食物和文公走散了，箕郑自己饿得头昏眼花，在路上哭，却不肯吃掉食物。这件事让晋文公很受感动，后来封箕郑做了原国的行政长官，文公认为箕郑永远不会背叛自己，大夫浑轩知道后对晋文公说了上面的话。

【译文】

作为明君，不要指望别人不会背叛自己，而要让别人不能背叛自己；不要指望别人不会欺骗自己，而要让别人不能欺骗自己。

明主之为官职爵禄也

An intelligent sovereign will create positions and rewards in order to choose talented people and encourage those of merit.

明主之为官职爵禄也，所以进贤材劝有功也。故曰：贤材者，处厚禄，任大官；功大者，有尊爵，受重赏。官贤者量其能，赋禄者称其功。

《韩非子·八奸》

An intelligent sovereign will create positions and rewards in order to choose talented people and encourage those of merit. Thus we can say, people with talent will hold high positions and be paid handsomely, while those of merit will be honored with great rewards. Officials will be judged according to their talents, and their salaries will be decided according to their merits.

【注释】

劝：勉励，奖励。《左传·成公十四年》："惩恶而劝善。"赋：授，给予。《国语·晋语四》："公属百官，赋职任功。"《吕氏春秋·分职》："出高库之兵以赋民。"注："赋，予也。"

【译文】

明君设置官职爵禄，是用来晋升贤材和奖励功臣的。所以说德才兼备的人受厚禄，做大官；功劳大的人受尊爵，有重赏。根据一个人的德才来任命他的官职，根据一个人的功劳来授予他俸禄。

明主之治国也，明赏，则民劝功

An intelligent sovereign governs a country by bestowing liberal rewards for good conduct . . .

明主之治国也，明赏，则民劝功；严刑，则民亲法。劝功，则公事不犯；亲法，则奸无所萌。

《韩非子·心度》

An intelligent sovereign governs a country by bestowing liberal rewards for good conduct and enforcing heavy punishments for crimes, therefore his people will strive to give meritorious service and abide by the law. If the people behave thus, the affairs of the state will be in order and crime will be suppressed.

【注释】
　　韩非子认为，以法治民旨在利民。利民的根本办法是不让他们为奸作乱，安于守法。守法则不生奸邪之心，所以韩非子说"禁奸于未萌"。萌：萌芽，引申为发生。

【译文】
　　明君治理国家，明定奖赏，民众就会努力立功；刑罚严厉，民众就会服从法令。民众努力立功，国家事务就不会受侵扰；民众服从法令，奸邪就不会产生。

母欺子，子而不信其母

If a mother cheats her child, her child will no longer have trust in her.

母欺子，子而不信其母，非以成教也。

《韩非子·外储说左上》

If a mother cheats her child, her child will no longer have trust in her. This is not the right way to educate a child.

【注释】

曾参的妻子上集市去，小儿子哭着要跟着去。母亲哄他说："你在家等着，我回来给你杀猪吃肉。"她从集市回来，曾参正准备杀猪，她阻止说："我不过是哄孩子不哭罢了，您怎么能真杀猪呀！"曾参说："小孩子才智尚不完全，要跟着父母的样子学习，完全听从父母的教诲。现在你欺骗了他，也就是教儿子学会了欺骗。做母亲的欺骗孩子，孩子就不相信母亲了，这不是教育孩子的正确方法。"于是就把猪杀了。

【译文】

做母亲的欺骗孩子，孩子就不相信母亲了，这不是教育孩子的正确方法。

目不明，则不能决黑白之分

Without the aid of keen eyes we cannot distinguish black from white.

目不明，则不能决黑白之分；耳不聪，则不能别清浊之声；智识乱，则不能审得失之地。

《韩非子·解老》

Without the aid of keen eyes we cannot distinguish black from white. Without the aid of sharp ears, we cannot differentiate between sounds. Without a discerning mind, we can not judge right from wrong.

【注释】

韩非子曰："视强，则目不明；听甚，则耳不聪；思虑过度，则智识乱。"意谓过分使用视力，眼睛就会不明；过分使用听力，耳朵就会不灵；思虑过度，智力的认识功能就会混乱。黑白：黑色和白色，也指是非善恶。

【译文】

眼睛不明，就不能判断黑白界限；耳朵不灵，就不能区别清浊声音；认识功能混乱，就不能弄清是非得失。

目失镜，则无以正须眉

We cannot groom our beards and brows without a mirror . . .

目失镜，则无以正须眉；身失道，则无以知迷惑。

《韩非子·观行》

We cannot groom our beards and brows without a mirror, nor can we discriminate between right and wrong without Tao.

【注释】

人的眼睛可以观察星宿，却看不见自己的睫毛、面容。所以古人发明镜子，就可以看清自己的面容。**迷惑**：迷乱，心神无主。《荀子·成相》："不觉悟，不知苦，迷惑失指易上下。"

【译文】

没有镜子，就没有办法整饰自己的胡须和眉毛；离开了道，就没有办法辨别是非。

能有其国、保其身者，必且体道

A person who can protect his country and himself will act in accordance with the basic principles.

能有其国、保其身者，必且体道。体道，则其智深；其智深，则其会远；其会远，众人莫能见其所极。

《韩非子·解老》

A person who can protect his country and himself will act in accordance with the basic principles. To do this, he must be profoundly wise. To be profoundly wise, he must attain great subtlety. To attain great subtlety, he must rise to a level well beyond the common man.

【注释】

韩非子曰："凡有国而后亡之，有身而后殃之，不可谓能有其国，能保其身。夫能有其国，必能安其社稷；能保其身，必能终其天年；而后可谓能有其国、能保其身矣。"**体道**：实行道。按照根本规律行事。体，实行，实践。《荀子·修身》："好法而行，士也；笃志而体，君子也。"《淮南子·泛论》："故圣人以身体之。"注："体，行。"**会**：计谋，谋算。

【译文】

能拥有国家、保全自身的人，一定会按照根本规律行事，他的智慧一定很深；智慧深其城府就深；城府深一般人就看不透他的根底。

千钧得船则浮，锱铢失船则沉

An object as heavy as a thousand kilograms can float on the water's surface with the help of a boat; yet without a boat, smaller things will sink into the water.

千钧得船则浮，锱铢失船则沉，非千钧轻而锱铢重也，有势之与无势也。

《韩非子·功名》

An object as heavy as a thousand kilograms can float on the water's surface with the help of a boat; yet without a boat, smaller things will sink into the water. It is not because the heavy object is light and the smaller things are heavy, but that they both need to draw upon the support of boats to succeed.

【注释】

千钧：三十斤为一钧，千钧即三万斤。常用来形容力量之大或器物之重。《商君书·错法》："乌获举千钧之重，而不能以多力易人。"锱铢（zīzhū）：锱和铢都是古代的重量计量单位，六铢为一锱，四锱为一两，这里指很轻的东西。

【译文】

千钧重物依靠船就能浮起来，锱铢轻物没有船就沉下水去；不是因为千钧轻而锱铢重，而是因为有没有依靠船的浮力这种"势"。

千丈之堤，以蝼蚁之穴溃

A dike of a thousand li can be destroyed by a single ant hole.

千丈之堤，以蝼蚁之穴溃；百尺
之室，以突隙之烟焚。

《韩非子·解老》

A dike of a thousand li can be destroyed by a single ant
hole; a building one hundred *chi* tall can be burnt down by
the sparks from a chimney.

【注释】

韩非子说："要想控制事物，就从细微处着手，所以老子说，'解决难题要从易处入手，想干大事要从小处开始。'" **蝼蚁**：蝼蛄和蚂蚁。**突隙**：烟囱的裂缝。突，烟囱。《淮南子·人间》："千里之堤以蝼蚁之穴漏，百寻之屋以突隙之烟焚。"

【译文】

千里长堤，因蝼蚁打的洞而导致溃决；百尺高屋，因烟囱裂缝漏出的烟火而导致焚毁。

去好去恶，臣乃见素

If the emperor does not reveal his preferences and dislikes, his ministers will reveal their true colors.

去好去恶，臣乃见素；去旧去智，臣乃自备。

《韩非子·主道》

If the emperor does not reveal his preferences and dislikes, his ministers will reveal their true colors. If the emperor abstains from disclosing his taboos and wits, his ministers will be self-restricted.

【注释】

去好去恶，臣乃见素：陈奇猷《韩非子集释》案曰，"《二柄》篇，'去好恶，群臣见素。'谓君无好恶，则臣不雕琢，不表异，而显露其质素。素，谓质朴而无文饰也。"去旧去智，臣乃自备：注曰，"好恶不形，臣无所效，则戒而自备。"旧，古读若"忌"。自备，约束自己。

【译文】

（君主）不表露好恶，臣下就会显出本相；除去忌讳，抛开智慧，臣下就会自行约束。

权不欲见，素无为也

The emperor should take a humble attitude to his power and not flaunt it wantonly.

权不欲见，素无为也。事在四方，要在中央。

《韩非子·扬权》

The emperor should take a humble attitude to his power and not flaunt it wantonly. He should assume the overall responsibility of a state and require his officials to manage their affairs.

【注释】

"扬权"就是弘扬君权。韩非子继承黄老学派思想，从哲学高度论证君权至高无上。提出君主应该和道一样以独一无二自居，高踞群臣和百姓之上。其中大权独揽、小权分散的原则今天尚有借鉴意义。见：同"现"。素：本色。无为：老子的哲学概念，是一种顺应自然的虚静状态。要（yào）：要点，纲要。唐·韩愈《进学解》："记事者必提其要。"

【译文】

君主不要随意显示自己的权力，而要经常保持一种虚静无为的心态。事务由各方官员去办，君主身居中央总揽大权。

人主不合参验而行诛

If a sovereign kills a man without investigation . . .

人主不合参验而行诛，不待见功而爵禄，故法术之士安能蒙死亡而进其说？奸邪之臣安肯乘利而退其身？

《韩非子·孤愤》

If a sovereign kills a man without investigation, or bestows rank and rewards upon those whom are without merit, then why would law enforcers be willing to risk their lives in presenting their ideas? Why would fraudulent ministers willingly discard their private advantages and withdraw from office?

【注释】

韩非子认为，君主宠信重臣而不信执法者是普遍现象。重臣得宠以进其奸，上迎合君心，下面又有党羽呼应。而执法者上言往往触到君主痛处，又遭群臣攻击，故多不能成事。其结果是"主上愈卑，私门益尊"。**参验：**用事实加以检验。

【译文】

君主不经验证核实就实行诛戮，不待建立功劳就授予爵禄，因此执法者怎肯冒死进忠言？奸邪之臣又怎肯面临有利可图的时机而自动引退呢？

人主者，非目若离娄乃为明也

A sovereign does not have to possess such sharp eyes as those of Li Lou's in order to be enlightened . . .

人主者，非目若离娄乃为明也，非耳若师旷乃为聪也。

《韩非子·奸劫弑臣》

A sovereign does not have to possess such sharp eyes as those of Li Lou's in order to be enlightened, nor does he have to possess such ears as those of the musician Shi Kuang's in order to be acute of hearing.

【注释】

"奸劫弑君"一篇旨在揭露奸邪权臣乱国窃权的种种伎俩。文中指出，如果君主不能以法治国，奸臣就会劫主弑君。韩非子曰："明主者，使天下不得不为己视，使天下不得不为己听。故身在深宫之中，而明照四海之内，而天下弗能蔽弗能欺者，何也？暗乱之道废而聪明之势兴也。"**离娄**：又称离朱，传为黄帝时人，以视力强著称。**师旷**：春秋时晋国著名乐师，善于辨音。

【译文】

做君主的人，视力不一定要像离娄那样才算明察；听力不一定要像师旷那样才算聪敏。

人主之道，静退以为宝

A sovereign's guiding principle of conduct must be to constantly remain self-possessed and humble.

人主之道，静退以为宝。不自操事而知拙与巧，不自计虑而知福与咎。

《韩非子·主道》

A sovereign's guiding principle of conduct must be to constantly remain self-possessed and humble. To be able to tell the difference between the skilful and unskilful managing of affairs by his ministers, without managing them himself; to perceive the success and failure of his ministers' proposals without making the proposals himself.

【注释】

静退：安静不露锋芒。静，安静。《墨子·非攻》："神民不违，天下乃静。"退，不为人先的意思。操事：操持事务。计虑：计划谋虑。咎（jiù）：过失，祸患。

【译文】

君主的原则，以安静退让为贵。不亲自操持事务而知道臣下办事的拙与巧，不亲自谋划事情而知道臣下谋事的成与败。

人主之患在莫之应

The anxiety of an emperor stems from an absence of response from his ministers, as he who stands alone has no power.

老人家说系列丛书

人主之患在莫之应，故曰：一手独拍，虽疾无声。人臣之忧在不得一，故曰：右手画圆，左手画方，不能两成。

《韩非子·功名》

The anxiety of an emperor stems from an absence of response from his ministers, as he who stands alone has no power. The anxiety of ministers lies in that they cannot ensure secure positions, as it is impossible for anyone to make a circle with one hand while simultaneously making a square with the other.

【注释】

莫之应：没有人响应。《老子》第38章："上礼为之而莫之应，则攘臂而扔之。"一：专一。《礼记·礼运》："欲一以穷之。"

【译文】

君主的祸患在于没人响应，孤掌难鸣。臣下的忧患在于不能专职，右手画圆，左手画方，不能同时成功。

仁者，谓其中心欣然爱人也

A benevolent person loves other people.

韩非子说

仁者，谓其中心欣然爱人也。其
喜人之有福，而恶人之有祸也。生心
之所不能已也，非求其报也。

《韩非子·解老》

A benevolent person loves other people, always rejoic-
ing in their good luck and lamenting their bad. They do so in
their innermost hearts with no expectation of repayment.

【注释】

生心：陈奇猷案曰："谓仁乃发生于心，不能自己。"

【译文】

仁者爱人，总希望别人有福，不希望别人有祸。这
是仁者自然生发于心的感情，而不是他们有意这样做以
期获得回报。

日月晕围于外，其贼在内

Though solar and lunar halos surround the periphery of the sun and the moon, they are formed from within them.

日月晕围于外，其贼在内，备其所憎，祸在所爱。

《韩非子·备内》

Though solar and lunar halos surround the periphery of the sun and the moon, they are formed from within them. Though people tend to guard against those they hate, conflict arises within their intimate circles.

【注释】

"备内"是说君主应防备宫内后妃、嫡庶诸子及权臣等弑君篡位。君主和后妃、诸子之间既是最亲近的人，又都存在着利害关系。韩非子曰："后妃、夫人、太子之党成而欲君之死也，君不死，则势不重。情非憎君也，利在君之死也。故人主不可以不加心于利己死者。"晕：日月周围的光圈。《史记·天官书》："日月晕适，云风，此天之容气。"集解引孟康："晕，日旁气也。"贼：伤害。《孟子·梁惠王下》："贼仁者谓之贼，贼义者谓之残。"备：防备。

【译文】

日月外围有白色光圈环绕，成因在于日月内部；防备自己所憎恨的人，祸害却来自自己所爱的人。

善任势者国安，不知因其势者国危

When a sovereign is skilful in holding his power, the country will be safe. When a sovereign is weak in maintaining his power, the country will be in danger.

韩
非子
说

善任势者国安，不知因其势者国危。

《韩非子·奸劫弑臣》

When a sovereign is skilful in holding his power, the country will be safe. When a sovereign is weak in maintaining his power, the country will be in danger.

【注释】

韩非子说："英明的君主，善于借用天下臣民的眼睛去看，善于借用天下臣民的耳朵去听。因此自己在深宫里，却能知道四海之内的真实情况，不会受人蒙蔽和欺骗，这是为什么呢？这是因为搞乱天下的阴谋被抛弃，聪明的权势被发挥。"**势**：权势。这里指"使天下不得不为己视，使天下不得不为己听"的"聪明之势"。

【译文】

（君主）善于发挥权势，国家就安定；不知道运用权势，国家就会出现危险。

赏莫如厚，使民利之

Rewards should not be otherwise than liberal, so that people will consider them beneficial.

赏莫如厚，使民利之；誉莫如美，使民荣之；诛莫如重，使民畏之；毁莫如恶，使民耻之。

《韩非子·八经》

Rewards should not be otherwise than liberal, so that people will consider them beneficial; honors should not be otherwise than prestigious, so that people will consider them noble; punishments should not be otherwise than strict, so that people will consider them severe; recriminations should not be otherwise than unbearable, so that people will consider them dishonorable.

【注释】

韩非子认为，人情有趋利避害的特点，法制就规定用爵禄之利来鼓励民众立功求利，用惩罚犯罪让民众避免灾祸。这样做，赏罚才能收到预期的效果。

【译文】

赏赐最好优厚，使民众得到实惠；表扬最好高调赞美，使民众感到荣耀；惩罚最好严厉，使民众感到畏惧；贬斥最好令人难堪，使民众感到羞耻。

赏无功之人，罚不辜之民，非所谓明也

It is unwise to reward men of no merit and to punish the innocent.

赏无功之人，罚不辜之民，非所谓明也。

《韩非子·说疑》

It is unwise to reward men of no merit and to punish the innocent.

【注释】

"说疑"是说君主要善于识别臣下各种难以辨认的阴暗迷惑行径。韩非子认为治理国家的重要问题，不仅仅是赏罚。赏无功，罚无罪，不能算是明察。赏有功，罚有罪，也不能从根本上起到建功止过的效果。

【译文】

奖赏无功的人，惩罚无罪的人，不能算是明察。

上有所长，事乃不方

If a sovereign always flaunts his talents, his ministers will be weak in handling their affairs.

韩
非
子
说

上有所长，事乃不方。矜而好
能，下之所欺。

《韩非子·扬权》

If a sovereign always flaunts his talents, his ministers will be weak in handling their affairs. If he is conceited and makes ostentatious displays, inept ministers will try to deceive him.

【注释】

韩非子认为君主治国应调动群臣的积极性，各尽其职各展其才。君主自己应该清静无为，垂衣而治。**上有所长，事乃不方**：君主展示自己的特长，臣下就会办事无当。方，当，适宜。《左传·闵公二年》："敬教劝学，授方任能。"注："方，百事之宜也。"**矜**（jīn）：自夸，自大。

【译文】

君主处处显示自己的特长，臣下办事就会无所适从。君主好自夸其能，臣下无能就会欺诈。

绳直而枉木斫，准夷而高科削

If the inked string is straight, crooked timbers will be shaved; if the water-level is even, high gnarls will be planed down.

绳直而枉木斫，准夷而高科削，权衡具而重益轻，斗石设而多益少。

《韩非子·有度》

If the inked string is straight, crooked timbers will be shaved; if the water-level is even, high gnarls will be planed down. Similarly, if weighing appliances are well calibrated, what is too heavy will be decreased and what is too light will be increased; once measuring tools are established, what is too great will be reduced and what is too little will be enlarged.

【注释】

韩非子认为，以法治国就是制定法令和保证其实行，就像有了墨线、水平器、称具和量具就能将曲木砍直，将（木材）高凸的部分削平，轻重多少，也就能平衡。**枉**：曲。**斫**（zhuó）：砍，削。**准**：测量水平的器具。**高科**：木材凸出的部分。**具**：同"悬"。**斗石**：斗和石都是容量单位，十斗为一石。

【译文】

有了墨线曲木就能被砍直；有了水平器，木材的高凸处就能被削平；有了称具就能减重补轻；有了量具就能减多补少。

圣人衣足以犯寒，食足以充虚

The saintly men, if they have sufficient clothes to resist the cold and sufficient food to fill their empty stomachs . . .

韩非子 说

圣人衣足以犯寒，食足以充虚，则不忧矣。

《韩非子·解老》

The saintly men, if they have sufficient clothes to resist the cold and sufficient food to fill their empty stomachs, have not a single worry.

【注释】

韩非子说："人不穿衣就不能御寒，不吃饭就不能生存，因此难免有欲利之心。欲利之心是自身的忧患，所以圣人穿衣只是为了御寒，吃饭只是为了充饥，除此之外就没有什么忧虑了。一般人却不是这样，大到诸侯，小到积存千金资财者，贪欲之心不能解除。因此说：'祸莫大于不知足'。"犯寒：战胜寒冷。犯，胜。

【译文】

圣人穿衣只为了能够御寒，吃饭只为了能够充饥，除此之外就没有什么忧虑了。

圣人执一以静

The enlightened sovereign remains in tranquility . . .

圣人执一以静，使名自命，令事自定。

《韩非子·扬权》

The enlightened sovereign remains in tranquility, allowing the able to appoint themselves to tasks and the affairs of state to settle themselves.

【注释】

执一以静：用道治国，清静无为。执一，专一。《荀子·尧问》："执一无失。"

自命：自正。《管子·法法》："政者，正也，正也者，所以正定万物之命也。"

【译文】

圣明君主虚静以待，让名义自正，事物自定。

圣人执要，四方来效

If the emperor holds his power firmly, officials from all directions will come to render him service.

圣人执要，四方来效。虚而待之，彼自以之。

《韩非子·扬权》

If the emperor holds his power firmly, officials from all directions will come to render him service. If he remains in a state of tranquility, they will exert themselves for him of their own accord.

【注释】

韩非子认为，弘扬君权是建立中央集权制国家的基础。君主自居中央保持独尊地位，掌握形名之术，控制赏罚大权。工作由各方官员去办。君主虚静以待，群臣就会各尽其能。以：用。

【译文】

君主独揽大权，四方官员就会竭力效劳。君主虚静以待，群臣就会各尽其能。

圣人之道，去智与巧

The way of an enlightened sovereign is to discard his scheming and tricks.

圣人之道，去智与巧，智巧不去，难以为常。民人用之，其身多殃，主上用之，其国危亡。

《韩非子·杨权》

The way of an enlightened sovereign is to discard his scheming and tricks. If his own scheming and tricks are not discarded, it will be hard for him to keep a constant principle of the government. If his officials and people do everything by sheer scheming and tricks, they will suffer losses; if the sovereign does so, the state will be in crisis.

【注释】

韩非子认为君主要谨慎运用治国之道，遵循自然规律，不要失去治国的要领，才能成为圣君。圣君治理国家不能靠自己的聪明与技巧，如果国君全凭自己的聪明与技巧，就很难维护国家的正常秩序。**去智与巧**：放弃聪明和技巧。《老子》第19章："绝圣弃智，民利百倍……绝巧弃利，盗贼无有。"又第65章："民之难治，以其智多。"

【译文】

圣明君主治理国家的方法，是要抛弃自己的聪明与技巧。如果不去掉聪明技巧，就很难维护国家的正常秩序。臣下和百姓要弄聪明技巧，自己就会吃亏；君主要弄聪明技巧，国家就会出现危机。

市之无虎也明矣，然而三人言而
成虎

It may be clear that there is no tiger in the market . . .

市之无虎也明矣，然而三人言而成虎。

《韩非子·内储说上》

It may be clear that there is no tiger in the market, nevertheless, if the rumor of the existence of a tiger was wildly spread, people will come to believe it.

【注释】

"储说"篇中，韩非子汇集和储存了很多历史故事和民间传说，用以阐述自己的法治观点，共分"内储说"和"外储说"两类。三人成虎：集市上本没有老虎，传言有虎的人多了，就信以为真。比喻谣言或讹传一再重复，即能蛊惑人心。庞恭陪太子到赵都邯郸做人质。临行前，庞恭对魏王说："有一个人说集市上有老虎，您相信吗？"魏王说："不相信。"庞恭说："有两个人说集市上有老虎，您相信吗？"魏王说："不相信。"庞恭说："有三个人说集市上有老虎，您相信吗？"魏王说："相信。"庞恭说："谁都知道集市上没有老虎，但是三个人的传言就造出了一只老虎。"庞恭是怕陪太子到赵国去之后，有人会在魏王面前说他的坏话。

【译文】

谁都知道集市上没有老虎，但是传言有虎的人多了，听的人就会信以为真。

事以密成，语以泄败

Affairs can succeed if they are kept secret, yet fail if they are divulged.

韩
非
子
说

老人家说系列丛书

事以密成，语以泄败。未必其身泄之也，而语及所匿之事，如此者身危。

《韩非子·说难》

Affairs can succeed if they are kept secret, yet fail if they are divulged. It is unnecessary for the participant to intend to expose any secrets; if he should happen to accidentally speak of anything the emperor wants to conceal, he will have placed himself in danger.

【注释】

韩非子说："有的君主表面上追求美名而实际上追求厚利，如果进言者用美名去说服他，他就会表面上接受而实际上疏远进言者；如果用厚利去说服他，他就会暗中采纳进言者的主张而表面上和进言者保持距离。"泄（xiè）：泄露。《管子·君臣下》："墙有耳者，微谋外泄之谓也。"匿（nì）：隐藏。《尚书·盘庚上》："不匿厥指。"

【译文】

事情因保密而成功，因谈话泄密而失败。未必是进言者本人泄露了机密，而是无意中触及了君主心中的隐匿的事，如此就会遭遇危险。

141

数披其木，毋使枝大本小

The branches of a tree should be trimmed often to avoid them growing larger than the trunk from which they stem.

数披其木，毋使枝大本小；枝大本小，将不胜春风；不胜春风，枝将害心。

《韩非子·扬权》

The branches of a tree should be trimmed often to avoid them growing larger than the trunk from which they stem. When the crown is large and the trunk is small, the tree will be unable to endure spring winds. If the branches grow wildly in the spring wind, the trunk will ultimately suffer greater damage.

【注释】

韩非子说："君主治理国家就像不断修剪树枝一样，要不断消除大臣的党羽，不使其滋生蔓延。树枝过分繁茂，树干就要承受更大的压力；大臣党羽泛滥，公门就会被堵塞，君权就会受到伤害。" **数披其木**：对树枝要经常修剪。数（shuò），多次，经常。披（pī），披折。**枝大本小**：树枝繁茂，树干细小。**不胜春风，枝将害心**：陈奇猷《韩非子集释》案曰："此以枝喻臣，以本与心喻君，春风喻时机。"

【译文】

树枝要经常修剪，不使枝权过分繁茂而影响树干的正常生长；树冠过大，树干过小，经不住春风送暖；春风一吹，枝权疯长，树干会受到更大的伤害。

树橘柚者，食之则甘，嗅之则香

The planter of orange and pomelo trees, upon eating and smelling the fruits obtains their sweet taste . . .

树橘柚者，食之则甘，嗅之则香；树枳棘者，成而刺人。故君子慎所树。

《韩非子·外储说左下》

The planter of orange and pomelo trees, upon eating and smelling the fruits obtains their sweet taste, while the planter of thorns and brambles will find the trees to be prickly when they mature. Thus, true gentlemen should be cautious when raising other men.

【注释】

鲁国季孙氏家臣阳虎发动叛乱失败后，逃到赵地。赵简子问道："我听说你善于栽培人。"阳虎说："我在鲁国时栽培过三个人，都做了令尹；在齐国时，我也推荐三个人做了官，但等我获罪后，没有一个人帮助我。"赵简子低头笑着说了上面的话。**橘柚**（júyòu）：常绿乔木。果实分别是橘子、柚子，味甜酸，有香味。**枳**（zhǐ）：落叶灌木或小乔木。茎上有刺，果实小而味酸苦，可入药。也叫枸橘（gōujú）。

【译文】

种植橘柚，吃起来是甜的，闻起来是香的；种植枳棘，长大了反而会刺伤人。所以君子栽培人时要慎重。

HAN·FEI ZI SAYS

水之胜火亦明矣，然而釜鬻间之

It is clear that water can overpower fire. Yet, when a pot comes between them . . .

146

水之胜火亦明矣，然而釜鬵间之，水煎沸竭尽其上，而火得炽盛焚其下，水失其所以胜者矣。

《韩非子·备内》

It is clear that water can overpower fire. Yet, when a pot comes between them, the water will heat and boil until it evaporates, while the fire will continue to burn with vigor beneath it, because the water will have lost the necessary conditions to extinguish the fire.

【注释】

韩非子说："以法治国是禁止奸邪的最好办法，但执法大臣却起到了锅那样的阻隔作用，法律只是在君主心里明白，却已经失去了禁奸的作用。"**釜鬵**（fǔ xín）：泛指锅类等炊具。《诗经·桧风·匪风》："谁能亨鱼？溉之釜鬵。"鬵，炊具，大釜。陈奇猷案："鬵作鬲。"亨：古烹字。

【译文】

水能灭火的道理再明白不过了，然而用锅把水和火隔开，水在上面沸腾以致蒸发完，而火在下面却烧得非常旺，这是因为水失去了灭火的条件。

虽无飞，飞必冲天

Though it has not flown for three years, once it starts flying it will soar high into the sky.

虽无飞，飞必冲天；虽无鸣，鸣必惊人。

《韩非子·喻老》

Though it has not flown for three years, once it starts flying it will soar high into the sky. Though it has not sung for three years, once it starts singing it will amaze all who hear it.

【注释】

楚庄王执政三年，不理政事，右司马用隐语对庄王说："一只鸟，落在南山上，三年不飞不鸣，大王知道这是什么鸟吗？"庄王说："三年不展翅，用来长羽翼；不飞不鸣，用来观察民情。虽然三年没有飞，一飞必冲天；虽然三年没有鸣叫，一鸣必惊人。"半年之后，庄王亲理朝政，除弊兴利，国势渐盛，后果然称霸诸侯。

【译文】

虽然三年没有飞，（可是）一飞必冲云天；虽然三年没有鸣叫，（可是）一鸣叫必然惊人。

所说出于为名高者也，而说之以厚利

If a person strives for fame while the advisor persuades him to pursue profit . . .

所说出于为名高者也，而说之以厚利，则见下节而遇卑贱，必弃远矣。

《韩非子·说难》

If a person strives for fame while the advisor persuades him to pursue profit, the advisor will be considered ill-bred and will incur indecorous treatment, and consequentially will be shunned and rejected.

【注释】

"说难"，指向君主进言的困难。战国后期，各诸侯国之间政治斗争、军事交战都十分激烈和复杂。各种政治团体和学派都想得到君主的支持，以推行自己的政治主张，但他们向君主进言的过程中却困难重重，有时还会遇到危险。韩非子认为进言者要想成功，必须根据不同情况，迎合君主的心理和要求，才能获得君主的信任。下节：节操低下。

【译文】

游说的对象追求美名，而游说者却用厚利去说服他，就会显得节操低下而受到卑贱的待遇，进而必然被抛弃和疏远。

所说出于厚利者也，而说之以名高

If a person strives for profit while the advisor persuades him to work for fame . . .

老人家说系列丛书

所说出于厚利者也，而说之以名高，则见无心而远事情，必不收矣。

《韩非子·说难》

If a person strives for profit while the advisor persuades him to work for fame, the advisor will be considered mindless and ignorant of worldly affairs, and will never be accepted and appointed to a high position.

【注释】

韩非子认为：向君主进言困难，不是难在进言者的才智不够和口才不好，也不是难在进言者有什么顾忌不敢把自己的想法表达出来，而是在于对君主的心理摸不透。**名高**：美名。**事情**：事实。《战国策·秦策二》："公孙衍谓义渠君曰：'道远，臣不得复过矣，请谒事情'。"注："情，实也。"

【译文】

游说的对象追求厚利，而游说者却用美名去说服他，就会显得没有头脑而又脱离实际，必然不会被接受和任用。

太山之功长立于国家

Only with the support of his people, an emperor's great achievements can stand eternally, like Mt. Tai.

太山之功长立于国家，而日月之明久著于天地。

《韩非子·功名》

Only with the support of his people, an emperor's great achievements can stand eternally, like Mt. Tai; his fame and prestige can forever shine gloriously upon heaven and earth like the sun and the moon.

【注释】

韩非子曰："古之能致功名者，众人助之以力，近者结之以成，远者誉之以名，尊者载之以势。"意谓君主功名的成就要靠万众一心的支持。**太山**：泰山。

【译文】

君主的丰功伟绩只有在万众一心的支持下才能像泰山一样建立起来，盛名威望才能像日月一样在天地间永放光芒。

天下有信数三

There are three truths under heaven . . .

天下有信数三：一曰智有所不能立，二曰力有所不能举，三曰强有所不能胜。

《韩非子·观行》

There are three truths under heaven: First, that even wise men find some tasks unachievable; second, that even strong men find some objects immovable; and third, that even brave men find some opponents invincible.

【注释】

韩非子认为人的智慧和才能各有其局限，明主应该知道自己的长处和短处，"以有余补不足"，顺应客观形势，找出成功的法则。信数：必然的道理。

【译文】

天下有三种必然的道理：一是智慧再高也有办不成的事情；二是力气再大也有举不起来的东西；三是实力再强也有打不赢的对手。

外举不避仇，内举不避亲

Recommend the right man who is competent, be he your family or your enemy.

外举不避仇，内举不避亲。

《韩非子·外储说左下》

Recommend the right man who is competent, be he your family or your enemy.

【注释】

晋平公让赵武举荐中牟县令，赵武说："邢伯子可以。"平公问："他不是你的仇人吗？"赵武说："私仇不涉及公事。"平公又让他举荐内库主管，赵武又举荐了自己的儿子。他这种"外举不避仇，内举不避亲"的精神境界，把对国家的负责和对人才的爱护有机地结合为一体，成为千古以来举荐人才的美德。

【译文】

举荐外人不回避自己的仇人，举荐自己人不回避自己的亲人。

惜草茅者耗禾穗，惠盗贼者伤良民

Whoever spares the weeds, hurts the crops; whoever tolerates thieves and robbers, injures good citizens.

老人家说系列丛书

惜草茅者耗禾穗，惠盗贼者伤良民。

《韩非子·难二》

Whoever spares the weeds, hurts the crops; whoever tolerates thieves and robbers, injures good citizens.

【注释】

晏子劝景公少用刑罚，韩非子认为晏子不考虑景公刑罚是否用得恰当，却拿刑罚太多劝说景公，这是很荒唐的。盲目减少刑罚，实行宽惠政策，实际上是便利奸邪而伤害好人，这不是治国的好办法。

【译文】

爱惜茅草便会损害庄稼，宽容盗贼便会伤害良民。

香美脆味，厚酒肥肉，甘口而疾形

Rich food and good wine are delicious to the palate, but they can damage the body.

香美脆味，厚酒肥肉，甘口而疾形；曼理皓齿，说情而捐精。故去甚去泰，身乃无害。

《韩非子·扬权》

Rich food and good wine are delicious to the palate, but they can damage the body. Beauty may please one's senses, but it will exhaust one's energy. Only when you avoid excesses and extremes of these, will you suffer no harm.

【注释】

疾形：使身体生病。疾，作动词用。形，身体。**曼理皓齿**：形容女人的美貌。曼理，细腻的肌肤。汉·张衡《七辨》："于是红华曼理，逸芳酷烈。"皓（hào）齿，洁白的牙齿。说：同"悦"。**捐**：耗费。**去甚去泰**：去其过甚。《老子》第29章："是以圣人去甚、去奢、去泰。"

【译文】

佳肴美酒，虽味道可口但损害身体；美貌佳人虽赏心悦目但耗费精力；因此对饮食美色要避免过量，才无害于身体。

削株无遗根，无与祸邻

If you leave no root when cutting down a tree, and be no neighbor to disaster . . .

削株无遗根，无与祸邻，祸乃不存。

《韩非子·初见秦》

If you leave no root when cutting down a tree, and be no neighbor to disaster, then disaster will not befall you.

【注释】

韩非子劝秦王用兵，并说："夫战者，万乘之存亡也。"意谓战争关系到一个大国的存亡。**削株无遗根**：砍树不留根。韩非子说：秦军曾大败楚军，如果乘势追歼楚军，就可以占领楚国，占领楚国之后，东可以削弱齐国、燕国，中原方面又可控制韩、赵、魏。果能如此，就可以一举成就霸主之名，可威服四邻诸侯。然而谋臣却不这样做，而是率秦军撤退，与楚国讲和，使楚国得以恢复沦陷的国土，聚集逃散的百姓，重立社稷，再建宗庙然后与各国联合攻秦。

【译文】

砍树不留根，不与祸患接近，祸患就不会存在。

刑当无多，不当无少

Punishments for crimes are not appraised by quantity, but by their equivalence.

刑当无多，不当无少。

《韩非子·难二》

Punishments for crimes are not appraised by quantity, but by their equivalence.

【注释】

晏子劝齐景公少用刑罚，韩非子认为刑不在多少而在适当。韩非子批评晏子不懂治国之道，他不是以刑罚不当告诫景公，而以用刑太多劝说景公，这是晏子不懂法度的表现。

【译文】

刑罚不在多与少，而在使用得是否恰当。

刑过不避大臣，赏善不遗匹夫

Punishments for crimes should never exclude ministers; rewards for merit should never pass over commoners.

刑过不避大臣，赏善不遗匹夫。

《韩非子·有度》

Punishments for crimes should never exclude ministers; rewards for merit should never pass over commoners.

【注释】

刑：处罚的总称。《尚书·大禹谟》："刑期于无刑。"过：过失。《尚书·大禹谟》："宥过无大，刑故无小。"《左传·宣公二年》："人谁无过？过而能改，善莫大焉。"大臣：古称官职尊贵者。《礼记·中庸》："敬大臣则不眩。"赏：对有功者赐予财物、官爵等。《尚书·泰誓下》："功多有厚赏。"匹夫：庶人，平民。

【译文】

惩罚罪恶不放过高官显贵，奖赏功劳不遗漏平民百姓。

刑胜而民静，赏繁而奸生

If penalties are strict, the people will keep public order; if rewards are too easily attained, wickedness will appear in society.

刑胜而民静，赏繁而奸生。故治民者，刑胜，治之首也；赏繁，乱之本也。

《韩非子·心度》

If penalties are strict, the people will keep public order; if rewards are too easily attained, wickedness will appear in society. Therefore strict penalties are the beginning of public order; easy attainment of rewards, the origin of chaos.

【注释】

韩非子指出，国之要务在于统一民心，而治民之本在于明法，使赏罚行于天下。他提出"治民无常，唯治为法"，"法与时转则治，治与世宜则有功"。行法的目的在于禁奸，奸禁则国治民安。

【译文】

刑罚严厉，民众就安定；赏赐太滥，奸邪就会滋生。所以治理民众，刑罚严是法治的首要任务，赏赐滥是造成国家混乱的根源。

虚静以待，令名自命也，令事自定也

Resting in emptiness and repose, the emperor manages everything so that all terms will define themselves and all affairs will be settled in themselves.

虚静以待，令名自命也，令事自定也。虚则知实之情，静则知动者正。

《韩非子·主道》

Resting in emptiness and repose, the emperor manages everything so that all terms will define themselves and all affairs will be settled in themselves. Keeping empty, he knows the truth of all matters. Being reposed, he understands the rule of action.

【注释】

虚静以待：虚无清静地对待一切。《韩非子·扬权》："圣人执一以静，使名自命，令事自定。"与此意同。《淮南子·主术训》："故云有道之主，灭想去意，清虚以待。"陈奇猷《韩非子集释》案曰："韩子所谓虚静，有其特殊之意义，非如老氏以无思无欲为虚静也。韩子不否认人有思虑有意欲，君主之思欲为国强位尊，臣民之思欲为离罚受赏。"**令名自命也，令事自定也**：陈奇猷案曰："为人主者，当以虚静处事，君不言其事，使为事者言之，君不定其事，使为事者定之。"

【译文】

（君主）虚无清静地对待一切，让万物依本质命名，让事情按规律发展。虚无才知道事物的真相，清静才知道行动的准则。

言赏则不与，言罚则不行

If neither rewards are bestowed as promised nor punishments carried out as sworn . . .

老人家说系列丛书

言赏则不与，言罚则不行，赏罚不信，故士民不死也。

《韩非子·初见秦》

If neither rewards are bestowed as promised nor punishments carried out as sworn, the guarantee of reward and punishment is of no faith, and soldiers will never be willing to risk their lives for the state.

【注释】

六国合纵攻秦，士兵却临阵脱逃，不肯死战。韩非子认为当时六国财库不满，粮仓空虚，却征发全国百姓，扩军数百万，光是戴羽冠的将军就不下千人，个个说决死战斗，尽管"白刃在前，斧锧在后，而却走不能死也"。韩非子认为士兵不肯死战，并非因为士兵怕死，是因为上面"赏罚不信，故士民不死也"。**言赏则不与：**说赏又不给。言，说话。不与，不给。**士民：**古代四民中学习道艺或习武勇的人。此处泛指征发作战的百姓。

【译文】

承诺奖赏却不给，说要责罚却不罚，赏罚失信，所以士兵不愿死战。

以乱攻治者亡，以邪攻正者亡

Failure is assured if a misgoverned country attacks a well-governed country; if a wicked country attacks a righteous country . . .

以乱攻治者亡，以邪攻正者亡，以逆攻顺者亡。

《韩非子·初见秦》

Failure is assured if a misgoverned country attacks a well-governed country; if a wicked country attacks a righteous country; and if a retrogressive country attacks a progressive country.

【注释】

"初见秦"是韩非子求见秦王的上书。韩非子通过对当时天下大乱形势的分析，赞扬秦国推行法治"号令赏罚，地形利害，在下莫若也"，指出秦国已具统一天下的条件。因以劝秦王用战争统一天下，建立统一的中央集权国家。**以乱攻治者亡**：以混乱的国家进攻安定的国家必定会失败。当时天下形势是六国合纵攻秦，韩非子认为这是"以乱攻治"、"以邪攻正"、"以逆攻顺"三种灭亡之道，六国都具备了。

【译文】

以混乱进攻安定必定失败，以邪恶进攻正义必定失败，以倒退进攻前进必定失败。

以尊主御忠臣，则长乐生而功名成

When a noble sovereign governs loyal ministers, a country's long-term peace and stability can be maintained and thus its success and good reputation can be achieved.

以尊主御忠臣，则长乐生而功名成。

《韩非子·功名》

When a noble sovereign governs loyal ministers, a country's long-term peace and stability can be maintained and thus its success and good reputation can be achieved.

【注释】

韩非子曰："人主者，天下一力以共载之，故安；众同心以共立之，故尊。人臣守所长，尽所能，故忠。"御：驾驭，使用。

【译文】

以尊贵的君主驾驭忠诚的臣子，就会出现长治久安的政治局面，功业和名望就能建立。

因可势，求易道

When dealing with affairs, one should seek favorable circumstances and the easiest path to success...

因可势，求易道，故用力寡而功名立。

《韩非子·观行》

When dealing with affairs, one should seek favorable circumstances and the easiest path to success, so as to accomplish great achievements through small efforts.

【注释】

因可势：顺应可以获得成功的形势。因，依靠，根据。《左传·僖公三十年》："因人之力而敝之，不仁。"也有随机应变的意思。《史记·老子韩非传》赞："老子所贵道，虚无，因应变化于无为，故著书辞称微妙难识。"求易道：寻找容易成功的条件。求，寻找，探索。《孟子·告子上》："求则得之，舍则失之。"

【译文】

（做事）顺应可获成功的形势，寻求容易取胜的条件，就能事半功倍。

用一之道，以名为首，名正物定

The way to govern a country begins with identifying the name in which to govern the country. When in the right name, the nature of things will become clear.

用一之道，以名为首，名正物定。

《韩非子·扬权》

The way to govern a country begins with identifying the name in which to govern the country. When in the right name, the nature of things will become clear.

【注释】

一：即道。《老子》第39章："昔之得一者：天得一以清，地得一以宁。"高亨注曰："本章诸'一'字，即道之别名也。" **名正物定**：名义正当，事物才能显出本来面目。《论语·子路》："子路曰：'卫君待子而为政，子将奚先？'子曰：'必也正名乎！'"孔子提出正名包括政治、伦理、社会等多方面内容。他正名的目的就是要实现"君君、臣臣、父父、子子"（《论语·颜渊》）的名分等级制度。孔子讲名指名分，韩非子讲名指名义，两者有所不同。

【译文】

君主治国之道应以正名为首，名正则事物本性就会显现出来。

有材而无势，虽贤不能制不肖

Without power and influence, even a talented sage cannot subdue the treacherous.

有材而无势，虽贤不能制不肖。

《韩非子·功名》

Without power and influence, even a talented sage cannot subdue the treacherous.

【注释】

韩非子认为势由位生，只有处于君位，才能握有权势。"故立尺材于高山之上，则临千仞之溪，非材长也，位高也。桀为天子，能制天下，非贤也，势重也；尧为匹夫，不能正三家，非不肖也，位卑也。" **材**：才能，才干。通"才"。《尚书·咸有一德》："任官惟贤材，左右惟其人。" **不肖**：不才，不正派。《商君书·画策》："不明主在上，所举必不肖。"

【译文】

有才能而没有权势，即使是贤人，也不能制服不正派的人。

有赏者君见其功，有罚者君知其罪

Of the rewarded, the emperor knows the meritorious service they rendered; of the punished, the emperor knows the criminal offence they committed.

老人家说系列丛书 韩非子说

有赏者君见其功，有罚者君知其罪。

《韩非子·难一》

Of the rewarded, the emperor knows the meritorious service they rendered; of the punished, the emperor knows the criminal offence they committed.

【注释】

韩非子认为，君主事先对群臣的功过了解得清清楚楚，然后进行赏功罚罪，就不会受蒙蔽。管仲不向桓公讲明这个道理，只是要桓公赶走三个佞臣，所以说管仲不懂法度。

【译文】

受赏的人，君主知道他的功劳；受罚的人，君主知道他的罪过。

輿人成輿，則欲人之富貴

When a cartwright finishes making carriages, he wants people to be rich and noble.

興人成與，则欲人之富贵；匠人成棺，则欲人之夭死也。非與人仁而匠人贼也，人不贵，则與不售；人不死，则棺不买。情非憎人也，利在人之死也。

《韩非子·备内》

When a cartwright finishes making carriages, he wants people to be rich and noble; when a carpenter finishes making coffins, he wants people to die early. Not that the cartwright is benevolent and the carpenter is cruel, but that unless people are rich and noble, the carriages will not sell, and unless people die, the coffins will not be bought. Thus, the carpenter's motive is not a hatred for people, but a realization that his profits come from people's deaths.

【注释】

興（yú）人：造车的工匠。匠人：技工。《墨子·天志上》："譬若轮人之有规，匠人之有矩。"指木工。夭（yāo）：少壮而死。《管子·形势》："贵有以行令，贱有以忘卑，寿夭贫富，无徒归也。"

【译文】

车匠造好车子，就希望人富贵；木匠造好棺材，就希望人早死。并不是车匠仁慈而木匠狠毒，（是因为）人不富贵，车子就卖不掉；人不死，棺材就没人买。（木匠）本意并非憎恨别人，而是他的利益就在人的死亡上。

智士者远见而畏于死亡，必不从重
人矣

The wise men, far-sighted and afraid of death, will never commit crimes out of obedience to high-ranking ministers.

韩非子说

智士者远见而畏于死亡，必不从重人矣；贤士者修廉而羞与奸臣欺其主，必不从重臣矣。

《韩非子·孤愤》

The wise men, far-sighted and afraid of death, will never commit crimes out of obedience to high-ranking ministers. Similarly, the honest men who are anxious to cultivate their personal integrity and would be ashamed of joining corrupt ministers in deceiving the sovereign will also never act in obedience to them.

【注释】

韩非子认为：君主的利益在于豪杰为国效力，臣下的利益在于结党营私。聪明人看得深远，怕犯死罪，必定不会跟从重臣犯罪；清廉的人洁身自爱，耻于和奸邪之人共同欺骗君主，也必定不会追随重臣犯罪。而跟随重臣犯罪的人不是愚蠢不知祸害的人，就是腐败而与奸邪同流合污的人。**重人：**即重臣，位高权重的人。

【译文】

聪明人看得深远，怕犯死罪，必定不会跟从重臣犯罪；清廉的人洁身自好，耻于和奸臣共同欺骗君主，也必定不会跟随重臣犯罪。

智术之士，必远见而明察

Men who are acquainted with the principles of governing a country are always prescient and clear-sighted.

老人家说系列丛书

智术之士，必远见而明察，不明察，不能烛私；能法之士，必强毅而劲直，不劲直，不能矫奸。

《韩非子·孤愤》

Men who are acquainted with the principles of governing a country are always prescient and clear-sighted. For, if not clear sighted, they cannot discern selfishness. Men who are able to uphold the law are always decisive and straightforward. For, if not straightforward, they cannot rectify wrongs and moral failings.

【注释】

智：同"知"，通晓。**烛私：**照见隐私。烛，照。《庄子·天道》："水静则明，烛须眉。"**矫奸：**纠正奸邪之人。矫，纠正。

【译文】

通晓治国之术的人，必定是远见卓识并能明察的人，不能明察，就不能洞察隐密私情；能推行法治的人，必定是坚决果断并刚强正直的人，不刚强正直就不能纠正奸邪之人。

智术能法之士用

If people who know how to govern a country and those who can uphold the law are appointed to governing posts . . .

智术能法之士用，则贵重之臣必在绳之外矣。是智法之士与当涂之人，不可两存之仇也。

《韩非子·孤愤》

If people who know how to govern a country and those who can uphold the law are appointed to governing posts, the ministers who usurp high positions will inevitably die off. This is the reason why they and the ministers in high positions are natural enemies, and unable to coexist.

【注释】

"孤愤"是韩非子孤独的愤慨。战国时韩国有两种政治力量针锋相对，维护君权追求法治的"智法之士"和结党营私盗窃国柄的"当涂之人"势不两立。**贵重之臣**：位尊权重之臣。这里指独断专行、无视法律的窃国之臣。**当涂之人**：指掌握重权的人。涂，同"途"，道路。也作"当路"。《孟子·公孙丑上》："夫子当路于齐，管仲晏子之功可复许乎？"**仇**：仇敌。

【译文】

懂得治国之术和能够推行法治的人被任用，那么窃国重臣必定为法律准绳所不容。如此说来，懂得以法治国的人和当权重臣是势不两立的仇敌。

众人多而圣人寡

The masses are many, the saintly men are few.

众人多而圣人寡，寡之不胜众，数也。

《韩非子·解老》

The masses are many, the saintly men are few. It is natural that the few cannot prevail upon the many.

【注释】

"解老"就是对《老子》的解释。这是中国哲学史上《老子》最早的解释专篇。《老子》又名《道德经》，全书共八十一章，分为上下两部分，是中国最早的哲学思想著作。**众人**：大家，一般人。**圣人**：有道之士。指具有方、廉、直、光四种德行的人。**数**：定理，必然的道理。

【译文】

一般人多而圣人少，少不能胜多，这是必然的道理。

主道者，使人臣有必言之责

The right way to be a sovereign is to make all ministers hold the personal responsibility for either giving their opinions ...

主道者，使人臣有必言之责，又有不言之责。

《韩非子·南面》

The right way to be a sovereign is to make all ministers hold the personal responsibility for either giving their opinions, or not giving their opinions.

【注释】

韩非子认为，君主治国的原则一是明法，二是责实，三是变古。明法就是彰明法度，使臣下不能违法专权。责实就是对臣下的言论和行为要循名责实。变古就是因时变法，反对守旧。**必言之责：**即有言之责。指人臣如果说话不负责任，无头无尾，花言巧语无从验证，就要追究其说话的责任。**不言之责：**指人臣如果遇事不表态，以保其地位，就要追究其不说话的责任。

【译文】

做君主的原则是，一定让臣下负起说话的责任，又要负起不说话的责任。

主利在有能而任官

The sovereign can benefit from appointing able men to office . . .

主利在有能而任官，臣利在无能而得事；主利在有劳而爵禄，臣利在无功而富贵。

《韩非子·孤愤》

The sovereign can benefit from appointing able men to office, while the minister can benefit from securing a high position with no competent abilities. The sovereign can benefit from awarding rank and rewards for distinguished services, while the minister can benefit from obtaining wealth and honor without merit.

【注释】

韩非子说："大国的祸患在于大臣权势太重，中小国家的祸患在于近臣太受宠信，这是君主的通病。君主和大臣的利益是不相同的。"利：利益。事：职务。《论语·卫灵公》："事君敬其事而后其食。"《韩非子·五蠹》："无功而受事，无爵而显荣。"劳：功绩。《周礼·夏官·司勋》："事功曰劳。"

【译文】

君主的利益在于对有才能者任以官职，臣下的利益在于没有才能而受到重用；君主的利益在于对有功劳者授以爵禄，臣下的利益在于没有功劳而得到富贵。

• 图书推荐 •
Highlights

"老人家说" 系列
Wise Men Talking Series

汉英 Chinese–English edition

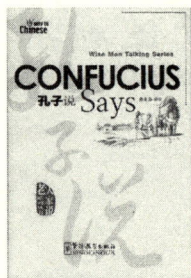

孔子说
Confucius Says
ISBN 9787802002111
201pp,145×210mm
¥29.80

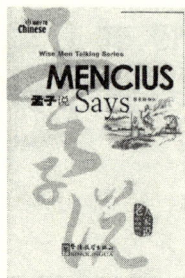

孟子说
Mencius Says
ISBN 9787802002128
201pp,145×210mm
¥29.80

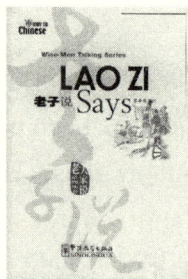

老子说
Lao Zi Says
ISBN 9787802002159
201pp,145×210mm
¥29.80

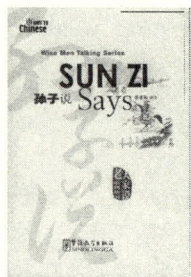

孙子说
Sun Zi Says
ISBN 9787802002142
201pp,145×210mm
¥29.80

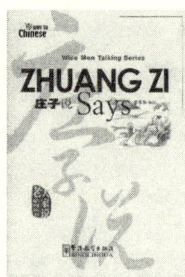

庄子说
Zhuang Zi Says
ISBN 9787802002135
201pp,145×210mm
¥29.80

For more information, visit us at www.sinolingua.com.cn
E-mail:hyjx@sinolingua.com.cn,　　**Tel:**0086-10-68320585,68997826

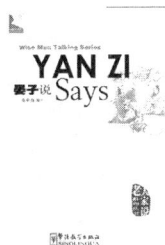

责任编辑：韩　颖
英　　译：韩芙芸
封面设计：胡　湖
印刷监制：佟汉冬

图书在版编目（CIP）数据

韩非子说：汉英对照／蔡希勤编注．—北京：华语教学出版社，2012
（老人家说系列）
ISBN 978-7-5138-0143-0

Ⅰ.①韩…　Ⅱ.①蔡…　Ⅲ.①汉语—对外汉语教学—自学参考资料②法家—汉、英　Ⅳ.①H195.4②B226.5

中国版本图书馆 CIP 数据核字（2011）第 161617 号

老人家说·韩非子说

蔡希勤　编注
*
ⓒ华语教学出版社
华语教学出版社出版
（中国北京百万庄大街 24 号　邮政编码 100037）
电话：(86)10-68320585　68997826
传真：(86)10-68997826　68326333
网址：www.sinolingua.com.cn
电子信箱：hyjx@sinolingua.com.cn
北京市松源印刷有限公司印刷
2012 年（大 32 开）第 1 版
（汉英）
ISBN 978-7-5138-0143-0
定价：35.00 元